Elemental

Elemental

NATURE-INSPIRED
RITUALS TO NOURISH
YOUR LIFE

Andi Eaton Alleman

Illustrated by Madeline M. Martinez

CHRONICLE BOOKS
SAN FRANCISCO

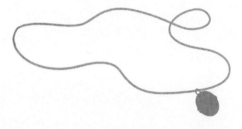

Library of Congress Cataloging-in-Publication Data available.

ISBN 978-1-7972-1430-6

Manufactured in China.

MIX
Paper | Supporting
responsible forestry
FSC™ C008047

FSC
www.fsc.org

Design by Angie Kang.
Illustrations by Madeline Martinez.

10 9 8 7 6 5 4 3 2 1

Chronicle books and gifts are available at special quantity
discounts to corporations, professional associations, literacy
programs, and other oganizations. For details and discount
information, please contact our premiums department at
corporatesales@chroniclebooks.com or at 1-800-759-0190.

Chronicle Books LLC
680 Second Street
San Francisco, California 94107
www.chroniclebooks.com

Contents

INTRO

Nature always wears the colors of the spirit.
—Ralph Waldo Emerson

Humans have always had an intimate connection to nature—we lived by the cycles of the sun and the moon, followed the flow of water when determining where to settle, and planted and sowed according to the shifts in seasons. By our very being, we are a part of nature.

Every single one of us has the opportunity to harness the power of nature to live healthier, more prosperous, and more joyful lives. When we treat our soul, spirit, and body equally, honoring the beauty that radiates from within, we glow differently. When we genuinely pay attention, observing the daily gifts the trees, flowers, lakes, and streams give to us, we learn to pause and find grounding.

Wellness shouldn't be complicated and should be available to everyone, no matter who you are, how much money is in your pocket, or where you are in the world. We have so much of what we need within, and the supporting tools can be sourced outside—in fields, forests, hills, valleys, rivers, and seas.

We're nourished holistically and wholly when we create synergy between ourselves and the natural elements. When we notice the sweetness of a summer breeze or the fog on a cool winter's day, we begin to dial in to a deeper connection.

Our daily news feeds bombard us with reasons to stress out at any given hour of the day. In this age of anxiety, committing time to truly disconnect from the world's digital speed, find balance, and reconnect with oneself is so needed.

Experts, coaches, and healers are urging us to find balance and a sense of calm by doing two things:

Looking inward, through mindfulness or meditation

Getting outside to experience the natural vibrancy of our surroundings

That's what this book is all about.

As our lives have become more urbanized over time, many people have experienced an increasing distance from nature. Think about why people sit in awe watching the sunset or trek to the countryside just to see the flowers bloom in spring. Regardless of age, gender, ethnicity, or culture, people are mesmerized by those little miracles that occur when we slow down and take in the natural world.

At its core, this book is about creating a lifestyle of radiant and natural living through communion with nature.

The five elements—fire, earth, water, air, and ether—reside in each of us and are the universe's building blocks. This book explores the energy and characteristics of each element and teaches how to incorporate a balance of each into your daily wellness practices. It's for wellness enthusiasts and novices alike, modern-day soul searchers, outdoor explorers, and natural beauty appreciators.

On the following pages, you'll find meditation and breath-work practices to amplify your glow, rituals for grounding and balance, and simple homemade recipes and exercises for nourishment. You'll learn how to make your own nature tool kits reflective of each element and ways to create nature-inspired sanctuaries at home.

MY STORY

My approach to living well is thoroughly enriched by exploring the five elements of nature through Ayurvedic wellness, yogic science and technology, and astrology.

I grew up spending my days in pine forests, weekends in the Appalachian Mountains, and summers on the dunes of the Carolina coast. My family was a quirky one. At home, my schooling in wellness came at an early age. My eighties aerobics instructor mother was a wellness practitioner in her own right before it was hip.

Aside from any trend, she taught me the value and simple joy of being outside. She was my coach, my cheerleader, and my friend. She encouraged me to find a sense of pleasure in exercise, mindfulness, and taking care of the flora and fauna in my home and neighborhood.

On sunny summer days, my friends and I would run down to the creek, pile up under a willow oak, and lean into the scratchy trunk—a natural conductor of the earth's energy—soaking up the vitamin D as we picnicked. We swam, climbed, frolicked, and dug in the dirt. In the evening, we'd come home exhausted but fully content.

I was a witchy child: collecting stones, shells, feathers for spells, and foraged flowers for jewelry, face coloring, and masks. I made blush from the flowers of dandelions, brewed herbs from the garden to wash my hair, and divined over stones and shells collected from the creek bed. I understood that I could feel energy in a different way than the kids around me. I had heightened perception and sensory experiences.

The best way I knew how to channel these feelings was to move. Movement awakens the creative spirit; it's meditation in its own right. It's an agent of freedom and exploration. Whether dashing through the woods or dancing in the kitchen to my parents' records, I found a sense of connection by tuning in to my body.

Years later, I got my first big job working for an Ayurvedic brand. The company—one of the first green beauty companies making products with plant and flower ingredients exclusively—had a stated mission to "care for the world we live in, from the products we make to the ways in which we give back to society." I spent over a decade studying natural approaches to wellness, Ayurvedic beauty, the science of aroma, and plant-based ingredients. I loved seeing what a difference using earthly ingredients can make for our health, fitness, and beauty.

After a decade working for the beauty brand I loved, I decided I needed to see what was next for me. So I packed only the essentials—my trusty Birkenstocks, a journal, a moonstone, and an astrology book—and booked a one-way trip to the Mediterranean.

I committed to lessening my footprint on the planet while cultivating an appreciation of the synergy between us (the people here on Earth), the natural world, and my cosmic connection. I spent my mornings meditating on the seaside; by night, I dove into celestial studies.

While exploring, studying the stars, and finding my way into yoga and meditation, I learned many lessons about myself, which I used to support my well-being. I discovered that holistic health, living beautifully and sensually, and pursuing healing are intertwined.

When we commit to growing our relationship with natural resources, we are all the better because of it. Getting outside and getting in touch with your sense of wellness is for everyone. You don't have to take the same leaps that I did to create a radiant, holistic lifestyle at home.

I started my blog *Oui, We*, a decade ago to document what I was experiencing personally. Today, *Oui, We*'s mission is to inspire confidence, self-worth, and well-being through holistic and experiential living, mystical thinking, and the art of the ritual. I'm honored to have created a space that's home to writers, educators, mystics, and wellness practitioners. The goal is to elevate resources that benefit the greater good and to empower people from all backgrounds.

My method incorporates yogic technology, psychology, cosmic alignment, and the science of human energy. In my practice, I'm a kundalini, lunar living, and manifestation teacher. Through my work, I've had the blessed fortune to connect and train with wisdom keepers: shamans, yogis, healers, astrologers, farmers, herbalists, conservationists, psychologists, and more.

I've studied with people who carry ancient traditions forward. It's encouraged my elemental approach to health. In these pages, I invite you to take what serves you and, as always, leave what doesn't behind. The beauty of these practices is that the more you tune in and listen to your inner wisdom and heart, the more quickly you'll find your own path to elemental well-being.

As you begin your practice, I encourage you to create your own rituals as you go. You'll learn what lights you up and what leaves you feeling balanced physically, mentally, emotionally, and spiritually. These practices are designed to guide you into a beautiful life, inside and out. Enjoy!

HOW TO USE THIS BOOK

Although you can dip into this book based on what speaks to you, I recommend that you work through it from start to finish and try each recommended exercise at least once. As you learn about each of the elements, you'll have an opportunity to explore practices in meditation, breathwork, movement, and ritual. The goal is to let your body speak and become an active listener to what it has to say. After a read-through, you'll be able to identify the rituals and practices that resonate with you most. Then, you can incorporate these practices into your life to support your overall wellness in whatever way feels the best to you.

Each elemental section opens with an affirmation. Affirmations can serve as magical little reminders, divine gifts to help us find alignment. Work with these affirmations in whatever way serves you: perhaps say them out loud to yourself in the mirror each morning, or allow them to vibrate through your mind as you sit in quiet meditation. You can use them as a screen saver or write them in your journal each evening before you go to bed. The practice of working with affirmations can help us make subtle mindset shifts.

Within each section, you'll find the rituals broken up into three main categories: Glow, Ground, and Nourish.

The Glow rituals are designed to increase vitality and physical well-being; you're encouraged through these rituals to invite Mother Nature to be your beauty cabinet. Learn to make concoctions and blends for infusing hair, skin, and body with natural radiance. The Glow rituals also include powerful breathing exercises designed to sustain and improve your life force energy.

The Ground rituals encourage an overall sense of peace and calm to reduce stressful feelings. Scientific evidence shows that when we live in contact with the earth's natural surface charge, we inherently feel better, physically and mentally. The Ground rituals include meditations to elevate your mood and leisurely ideas for exploring your natural surroundings.

The Nourish rituals celebrate a holistic approach to taking care of ourselves from the inside out. Find simple, calming recipes for teas, tonics, and elixirs, as well as special exercises and daily practices to infuse energy into the body while cultivating a deeper connection to nature's gifts.

If you're not sure which element to focus on first, you can start by taking the What's Your Elemental Constitution Quiz on page 20 to gain insight into your natural elemental constitution. Keep in mind that our bodies and our emotional and spiritual states of being are in constant flux, so even once you've discovered your elemental makeup, that doesn't mean there won't be uses for the practices and rituals in the other sections. The quiz isn't a one-time-only determination—take it regularly to see what resonates with you at different points in your life.

Here are a few additional recommendations on ways to incorporate these practices:

Seasonal Harmony

Each element is associated with a season, so you can work through that element's practices to align your energies with that season. For example, in the Fire section, Breath of Fire (page 45) could be practiced in the summer (the season of fire) to inspire inner power and action. Alternatively, if you're interested in finding more balance, choose a practice from the element opposite of the current season to recalibrate.

Cosmic Attunement

Each element is also associated with a lunar phase, an astrological sign, and a planet, so you can choose practices from the element in alignment with astrological or planetary activity. For example, practice the Fire-Releasing Ritual (page 52) during a full moon, enjoy a Goddess Bath (page 116) during Venus Retrograde, or explore Forest Bathing (page 82) during earthy Taurus season.

Geographic Alignment

Another way you can incorporate these practices is based on geographic location. For example, consider fire or water practices when you're exploring places with warmer climates, like the desert or tropical islands, or try air practices when you're traversing mountains or hills. Like the seasonal harmony approach, if you find you're out of balance, choose exercises from the element opposing your current climate. For example, if it's snowing outside and you're interested in warming up from the inside, try Candle Gazing (page 51) and a trip to the sauna.

PREPARING FOR YOUR PRACTICE

While some of the rituals in this book call for simple ingredients you can find at your farmers' market, local grocer, or health food store and others necessitate essential tools like a comfortable setup for meditation, many of the practices require nothing more than you and your willingness to show up for yourself.

My number one recommendation? Simply begin.

If you're engaging with this book at home, it's nice to set up a dedicated space for your practice. A few things, such as a meditation cushion, a plant-based candle, and crystals, can turn even a small corner into an oasis.

In addition, many spirit tools can enrich and transform your state of being when you understand how they work, their potency, and how to use them in your ritual practices. Each element section has a nature tool kit that offers suggestions for items to add to your space to further align with that element.

The tool kits recommended for each element are compilations of mood-enhancing herbs, woods, plants and flowers, gemstones, rocks, spices, found and foraged items, and other spirit tools that precisely align with that particular chapter's element. These items have been used ceremonially in different parts of the world, so be mindful and respectful of the history and traditional uses of your items.

When I was gifted my first bundle of palo santo, I was quickly drawn to the wafts of streaming smoke and the woodsy scent. The aroma gave me a mood boost immediately. That first bundle didn't come with the details of the scientific evidence explaining why I instantly felt lifted (it contains antioxidant-rich phytochemicals with healing properties) or a history lesson outlining the traditional rituals practiced by Indigenous people (indigenous to Mexico, Ecuador, and Peru, palo santo has been burned by medicine men and women and shamans for centuries). All I knew was that the smell permeated the room and seemed to fill me up with a sense of calm.

As you begin to practice rituals and personal ceremonies and to gather the items for your own nature tool kits, make sure you're doing your research to buy high-quality, ethically cultivated items. Shaman markets or local herbal shops are good places to start. Unfortunately, many online stores aren't concerned with selling high-quality ceremonial and ecologically responsible products, so treat your medicinal plants as you do your food: Shop organic and from a local source. In addition to being mindful when sourcing sacred herbs, smokes, crystals, and spirit tools, make an effort to educate yourself on their historical origins before using them. Herbalist, medicine maker, and educator Adriana Ayales offers workshops, tools, and a newsletter packed with resources through her shop Anima Mundi Apothecary. The commodification of white sage, for example, has created concern that it's being overharvested and has contributed to a loss of respect for Native American religions and rituals.

Once you've gathered your tool kit items, you can use them in many ways; for example, create mini altars around your home, bring them into your rituals and meditations, or carry the items with you for protection and cleansing.

Each of us deserves an opportunity to feel our best. At the same time, we owe it to our planet to consider ways to support nature's recovery and regeneration and restore health and well-being to both people and the earth.

Elemental well-being—the core of this book—is about creating a more substance-filled life.

I encourage you to make notes about your practices, to keep a record of the recipes and rituals you've tried, and to dive deeply into your psyche while supporting your physical well-being. Journaling is a beautiful way to document small shifts and ultimately your transformation as you embark on a lifetime of elemental well-being.

WHAT'S YOUR ELEMENTAL CONSTITUTION?

Take this quiz to discover your current natural elemental constitution. Tally up your responses for each letter, and reference the key at the end of the quiz to see where to begin.

Keep in mind that your body, mind, and spirit can change based on external environmental factors and your internal state of being, so answer the questions based on how you're feeling *today*, and come back to take it regularly to see what resonates at different times in your life.

1. I would describe my typical energy level as:

A. Sporadic: I tend toward extremes; my energy comes in waves.

B. Low: I'm sometimes lethargic and apathetic, and I need lots of rest and recharge time.

C. Slow but constant: It takes a lot to get me going, but I can be stimulated by my surroundings.

D. High: I have an abundance of energy and sometimes can't settle down.

E. Consistent: I feel steady most of the time; I enjoy taking action and resting equally.

2. My stress response is most often:

A. Anger: I become irritable and hot-tempered easily but can often find calm just as quickly.

B. Withdrawal: I consider myself a peaceful person and need alone time when something troubling happens.

C. Sadness: I tend to feel deeply emotional in stressful situations.

D. Anxiousness: I'm prone to worrying about things beyond my control.

E. Nervousness: I'm exhausted and overwhelmed by too much stimulation.

3. My beauty cabinet is always stocked with:

A. Sunscreen and cooling masks: My skin is delicate and inflammation prone; it burns the second I step into the sun.

B. Glow serums and spot treatments: My skin gets oily in the T-zone, with the occasional breakout.

C. Foam cleansers and exfoliants: My skin is shiny, sometimes oily, and prone to blackheads.

D. Anti-aging and brightening serums: My skin can be sallow and matte; I have fine lines and wrinkles.

E. Moisturizer and facial oils: My skin is occasionally dull with dry patches.

4. Describe your general body temperature:

A. Hot weather makes me feel worn out and drained; I sweat easily and notice I'm usually warmer than people around me.

B. I adapt easily to most climates, but when given a choice, I prefer cooler weather.

C. Cool, damp weather chills me to the bone; I prefer dry heat, and I wear layers to stay comfortable.

D. I dislike cold, dry weather but thrive in warm humidity; I often need a sweater when other people don't.

E. I'm comfortable in temperate environments, though I prefer keeping the thermostat on the warmer side.

5. Describe your sleep patterns:

A. I'm a sound sleeper; once I fall asleep, I don't wake up often. I usually get at least 6 hours of sleep.

B. I'm a heavy sleeper and frequently feel groggy and sluggish when I wake up; I'd get over 8 hours a night if I could.

C. I'm a deep sleeper and require at least 7 or 8 hours of sleep to feel my best in the morning.

D. Sleep is elusive for me; I have frequent insomnia.

E. I'm a light sleeper; I have trouble falling asleep and awaken easily.

6. Describe your approach to daily routine:

A. Sometimes my physical and mental energy comes in bursts. I love a daily game plan to stay on task and focused.

B. My style is slow, precise, and methodical. Consistency helps keep me motivated.

C. I thrive with rituals and routines in place; I feel most effective, efficient, and grounded when following a detailed calendar and to-do list.

D. I'm averse to to-dos and task lists but thrive and feel inspired when I embrace spontaneity; I'm sometimes late or miss appointments.

E. I'm not a fan of schedule and structure. When I follow intuition and go with the flow, I move through daily activities quickly and with ease.

7. Describe your mental engagement style:

A. I'm highly intelligent and retain information easily; however, my moods and passions can change quickly, and I sometimes lose focus.

B. I'm often slow to learn new things; however, I'm methodical and retain information for the long term well. Once I've acquired a new skill, I work toward mastery.

C. Making decisions and commitments can be hard for me; I take a little longer to absorb new information. Sometimes it feels like it's in one ear and out the other.

D. I'm a fast learner but am often forgetful and have trouble recalling short-term memories.

E. I have a sharp intellect, am often quick-witted, and actively seek out new information. Rote memorization, on the other hand, is difficult for me.

8. Others have described my personality as:

A. Passionate, lively, and determined

B. Steadfast, stable, and loyal

C. Patient, artistic, and intuitive

D. Creative, gifted, and innovative

E. Inspiring, enlightened, and influential

9. My natural body type is:

A. Proportionate: I have moderate muscle development with regular exercise.

B. Athletic: I'm solid and strong.

C. Supple: I'm curvy and my body weight can fluctuate depending on my routine.

D. Airy: I'm petite and smaller boned, with lean muscle tone.

E. Angular: I'm long, slender, and have minimal muscle tone with regular exercise.

10. My movement style could be described as:

A. Enthusiastic: I enjoy high-intensity interval training and have regular bursts of energy.

B. Slow and steady: I enjoy hiking and trail running.

C. Fluid: I love activities like synchronized swimming and ecstatic dance.

D. Vigorous: I love aerobic activities like cycling and running.

E. Buoyant: I love mind-body systems like yoga and Pilates.

If you've chosen mostly As, explore Fire (page 36).
If you've chosen mostly Bs, explore Earth (page 62).
If you've chosen mostly Cs, explore Water (page 92).
If you've chosen mostly Ds, explore Air (page 120).
If you've chosen mostly Es, explore Ether (page 148).

If you have several elements that are close in score, read through each chapter and decide which practices resonate the most with you today.

PART 1

ELEMENTAL FUNDAMENTALS

In our most "well" state, our bodies and minds are tuned in to and aligned with the natural world. The study of natural elements and their relation to wellness is present in Chinese medicine, ancient Greek philosophy, shamanic practices, Ayurveda, astrology, Wiccan spirituality, and more. The teaching across these schools of thought is that all living things in the universe are composed of elemental building blocks.

When we incorporate the elements into our daily lives as tools to optimize our health and well-being, we have the potential to truly thrive from a mind, body, and spirit perspective.

As a yogi, a practitioner of Ayurveda, and a modern mystic, I speak only from my experience. I hope to bring ancient wellness practices and technologies I've learned from my teachers and transformative approaches to working with nature's offering into this current moment with grace, ease, approachability, and humility.

You'll see three technologies repeated throughout this book: yogic technology, Ayurveda, and astrology. Each includes the practice of working with elements within its framework. Here are some basics on each.

YOGIC TECHNOLOGY

Yoga is a powerful method for transformation, both internally and externally, and an incredible tool for balancing elemental energies within the body. Yogic technologies, including hatha, vinyasa, and kriya yoga components, come from oral tradition, passed directly from teacher to student.

These practices support our overall well-being, including our fitness and mindset, and they help align our chakras—our spiritual energy centers. Each chakra corresponds to specific senses, emotions, and physical states of being.

Patañjali, an Indian sage, collated this oral tradition into his classical work, the *Yoga Sutras*, a two-thousand-year-old treatise on yoga philosophy. The *Yoga Sutras* offers the framework upon which all yoga practiced today is based. It offers spiritual advice and guidance on how to master the mind and emotions.

In this book, our elemental practices include the technologies of pranayama, mudras, mantra, and asanas.

Pranayama, or breath control, is a central component of yoga. Pranayama is the science of breath, a form of energy management to support health, consciousness, and emotional states. The ability to consciously control your breath will allow you to move through challenging situations with grace. Regarding the elements, we're able to introduce fire and heat, or to cool the body, through different approaches to breathwork.

Mudras are beautiful symbolic hand gestures that serve as a map to the mind-body energy system. Each area of the hand links a particular area of the body to different emotions and behaviors. Mudras often also correlate to planetary energy. Each element corresponds to a planet; there is an opportunity to balance elemental energy by simply working with your hands.

Mantra (from the Sanskrit for "sacred message") is the practice of working with sound to affect consciousness. Mantras are vibrations—everything in this world, down to the subatomic level, is in constant motion, a vibrational frequency. This vibration is pure energy. Chanting mantras is an ancient practice that aligns our day-to-day thoughts with our higher calling. It's a proven practice for calming the mind; scientific studies have found that chanting a mantra like "om" for 10 minutes can ease feelings of anxiety and depression.

Asanas—yoga postures or meditative poses—are prescribed for various intended outcomes, some to reduce stress levels, others to increase energy, flexibility, or strength. Practicing a variety of asanas can help you elevate your state of consciousness.

When you begin to integrate breath, posture, sounds, and hand positions in rhythmic patterns and sequences (known as a kriya in kundalini yoga), you can begin to alter your physical, emotional, and mental experience. Depending on your imbalances, challenges, and subconscious patterns, practicing various breathing techniques, meditations, asanas, and kriyas will improve your well-being.

In this book, I invite you to explore each of these yogic technologies to discover what aligns with you. I often say in my workshops: Sometimes, when we're feeling resistance to a particular meditation, or kriya, for example, it's the one we need most. When practicing yoga, always take care to notice when you're feeling uncomfortable (which is okay) versus when you're in pain (which is not).

Discomfort can often help us move through blocks while finding a renewed sense of confidence and power. When working to replace old conditioning, challenge yourself to explore a new, more desirable frequency through repetition. Notice the physiological shifts that occur when you set this sort of practice in motion.

AYURVEDA

Ayurveda ("the knowledge of life" in Sanskrit) is an ancient Indian system of holistic healing, well-being, and balance. With a spotlight on total body wellness and a preventative approach to healing, Ayurveda works to harmonize our internal and external realms. It's a practice of cleansing, detoxifying, and nourishing the body from the inside out.

The five elements—fire, earth, water, air, and ether—are present in everything and influence how our bodies function. In Ayurveda, everything we experience, from physical sensations to emotional states of being, have specific qualities, also known as the doshas. The three Ayurvedic body types, or doshas, are vata (a combination of air and ether), pitta (a combination of fire and water), and kapha (a combination of earth and water). When our doshas are balanced and our elements are in equilibrium, we look and feel our best. To begin incorporating the practices in this book into your life, consider starting with a morning ritual routine (a dinacharya: *dina* meaning "day" in Sanskrit and *charya* meaning "to follow a routine"). This is a beautiful way to begin to balance the dosha s and to invite your body to align with nature's rhythms.

ASTROLOGY

Birth charts, the "big three," planetary transits, and retrogrades are starting to become part of day-to-day conversation (see page 166 to learn more about studying your astrological chart). But what exactly is astrology? Astrology is the study of the connection between celestial phenomena and earthly events. Astrology ascribes meaning to the placement of the sun, the moon, and the planets in relation to regions where well-known constellations appear. In astrology, each astral body aligns with the twelve signs of the zodiac named for those constellations.

Each of the twelve zodiac signs is associated with one of four elements: fire, earth, water, and air. The qualities of these elements directly relate to the characteristics of each sign. In astrology, fire energy is dynamic, passionate, heartfelt, and restless. Earth energy is tactile, material, rooted, and sensual. Water energy is mysterious, sensitive, emotional, and devoted. Air energy is conceptual, cerebral, mercurial, and communicative.

Our natal charts are much more than our big three: our sun, moon, and rising signs. For example, you can have a fire sign as your sun sign; however, if your other inner planets (Mercury, Venus, and Mars) and the moon—the celestial bodies said to have the highest direct impact on our composition, personalities, and day-to-day experiences—have higher concentrations in water, earth, or air signs, you may find it worthwhile to incorporate the practices for those secondary elements to provide balance for your sun sign's energy.

The study of astrology has been around in various forms for thousands of years. Ancient Greeks began mapping the stars and naming the constellations that we still reference today. Many students of astrology (including me!) believe we're globally transitioning into the constellation of Aquarius or the Age of Aquarius. Aquarius, "the cupbearer," was documented in the second century by astronomer and mathematician Claudius Ptolemy. Aquarius is a sign of community spirit, hope, and innovation.

While our planet moves from constellation to constellation, influencing global energies, your individual birth chart can show you, in relatively unambiguous terms, how you might personally experience the world. In this book, I encourage you to consider the influence of your planetary placements and the elemental connections to astrological connection as a methodology for choosing practices to balance each element within your energetic makeup.

PART 2

THE ELEMENTS

I ACT WITH COURAGE, STRENGTH,
AND CONFIDENCE IN ALL THAT I DO.
I AM THE LIGHT OF MY SOUL.

Fire is a force—divine and living, it resides within us all. It's the ultimate trans- former, ensuring that change is inevitable in everything that exists. All forms of change—physical, mental, emotional, and spiritual—are dependent on fire. Its presence can be intoxicating, relaxing, and thera- peutic. In both ancient and modern times, building fire is mission-critical to survival.

In yoga traditions, fire is *shakti*, the creative energy of the divine. At the level of individual consciousness, fire expresses itself as the indomitable power of will and determination. Fire is associated with bold living—it invokes enthusiasm, passion, vitality, courage, charisma, spontaneity, strength, and high spirits.

Fire drives us toward the fulfillment of our dharma, or truth. Those with a higher concentration of fire in their energetic constitution know a thing or two about creating a vision and aiming for what is believed to be possible and beneficial. That doesn't mean that you can't cultivate vision and passion if your natural makeup doesn't include as much fire; it simply means it's up to you to cultivate more fire. Fire energy lights us up, driving our capacity for inspired action-taking upward.

When our fire energies are balanced, we may notice feelings of positive intensity, strong will, power, boldness, and bravery. When we're experiencing the shadow side of fire, we may notice feelings of frustration, irritability, impa- tience, anger, and rage.

Fire's energy is most pronounced in warm climates and high kinetic energy centers, like tropical locales, vibrant cities, and desert sand dunes lit up by blazing sunsets. To bring more fire into your life, explore locations like these to inspire lively artistic ambition and powerful creative expression.

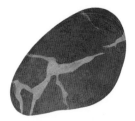

THE FIRE ELEMENT

ARCHETYPE

Royal, Warrior, Explorer

SEASON

Summer

The summer solstice officially marks the start of summer, ushering in the longest days of the year. A heat falls upon us as we're lit up by the fiery luminary in the sky, the sun. As we embrace the physical light, we are encouraged to embrace and celebrate our inner light and the essence of who we truly are.

LUNAR PHASE

Full Moon

Full moons occur when the moon and sun are opposing each other in the sky, shining light and illuminating areas in our lives that may require evaluation or change. Our manifestation energy and magnetism peak during the full moon phase. The power of this lunation amplifies creativity and action.

CELESTIAL BODY

The Sun

The sun is the giver of life, representing our life force and conscious mind. Just as each planet in our solar system circles it, the sun represents our ego and soul fire within. It represents our basic identity, self-realization, and overall vitality.

DIRECTION

South

South is the direction of the sun at its highest point in the sky, noon on the clock. It is the place of summer, of fullness, of youth, of physical strength and vigor.

ASTROLOGICAL SIGNS

Aries, Leo, Sagittarius

Fire can give life or take it away—it's completely transformative and moves with high energy and rapid pace. Fire can create or destroy, and the astrological signs associated with it demonstrate the intensity of these traits. The fire signs are often charming and outwardly passionate individuals. They exude spontaneity, inspiration, and a competitive spirit.

SENSE

Sight

Fire provides the light for perception. The eyes are the channel through which light is absorbed and perception takes place.

NATURE TOOL KIT

ANYTHING THAT
EVOKES YOUR
PASSION, PIQUES
YOUR CURIOSITY, OR
OTHERWISE CAUSES
A SPARK IN YOU

CANDLES

GARNET

RED JASPER

MATCHES

CINNAMON STICKS

CARNELIEN CRYSTAL

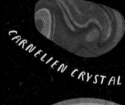

CLOVES

CITRUS FRUIT

GINGER OR
THISTLE TEA

GLOW

AFFIRMATION

I am purified and renewed. I dispel darkness
and light up my soul from within.

Fire is nature's transformer. Associated with alchemy,
strength, and the radiance of the sun, these practices
support a transition of consciousness through breath,
uplift our mood, flush out toxins, and align us to the
rhythm of nature.

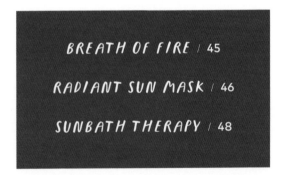

Breath of Fire

Breath of fire, or kapalabhati pranayama, is a yoga practice of purification. The word *kapalabhati* is made up of two Sanskrit words: *kapāla* ("skull") and *bhāti* ("illuminating"). I began practicing breath of fire years ago as a fundamental breathing technique in my hot yoga sequence; my teacher would guide the class into and out of our session with a minute of this technique.

As I explored additional yoga modalities, hatha and then kundalini, I found this breath to be integral to the practice and one that provides remarkable benefits. This breathwork practice is calming, detoxifying, and strengthening, and is known to create healing and take the practitioner into higher planes of consciousness.

Breath of fire begins at the solar plexus, the third chakra (see page 29 for more information on chakras). It works by pumping from the center of the navel while you breathe rapidly, rhythmically, and continuously through the nose. The goal is to generate heat within the body and burn off negative karma held in the solar plexus chakra, which is the emotional center of the chakra system. It helps to balance our inner fire as we focus attention on the space between the navel and the heart.

This particular point in our bodies connects to our self-confidence and self-acceptance. The inner glow we nurture through this practice impacts the quality of our relationships with both ourselves and others.

Activating the solar plexus chakra challenges you to have the willpower, the inner fire, to make positive choices that enhance your life. This practice will spark courage and conviction as you dial up your inner power.

This breath can be intense—if you feel lightheaded while practicing, stop and rest. If this is your first time, ease into it by beginning with 30 seconds and working up to 3 minutes or more.

Sit up tall so that your airways are open and clear. Warm up with three long, deep breaths.

Begin by breathing with force, exhaling through your nose, forcing air out, and contracting your navel inward. Imagine that you're blowing into a tissue. The power of the exhale will result in a natural, passive inhale.

Seal your lips, and continue the vigorous exhale through your nose, followed by a relaxed inhale, feeling your navel begin to rise in a pumping motion. Your upper abdominal muscles will continue to pull in and up. This will begin to feel automatic as you contract your diaphragm rapidly.

As you continue to practice, you'll notice a rhythmic pace within your breath; keep your body relaxed, focus on relaxing your hands and arms, feet and legs, face, lips, head, and torso.

Keep your eyes closed and hold your gaze at your third eye.

Radiant Sun Mask

I spent years of my career working for an Ayurvedic beauty brand; at that time there were very few luxury brands made with clean ingredients. The brand I worked for focused on haircare, and after years of training, I was inspired to create a skincare regimen for myself that would align with the Ayurvedic rituals and practices I was learning in my work.

This mask is designed to give your skin a warm, radiant glow with two magical ingredients: turmeric and saffron. It's especially great for those with acne or rosacea, redness, or sensitive skin. Both turmeric and saffron provide anti-oxidant power, are soothing anti-inflammatories, and encourage circulation. Yogurt and honey offer gentle exfoli-ation and hydration. In combination, these ingredients help create a natural glow.

A diet of ultra-processed foods, harsh chemicals in our skin-care products, and too much sun can dramatically increase the free radical production in the body, and over time, the skin can begin to show discoloration.

With the Radiant Sun Mask, turmeric checks free radicals before they can do damage, and saffron can encourage exfoliation and a resurfacing effect. Saffron is also said to stimulate collagen and elastin production, giving the skin a well-toned and supple feel.

HOW TO MAKE IT

½ cup plain organic yogurt (dairy or nondairy)
2 Tbsp raw honey
2 strands of saffron
¼ tsp turmeric

In a medium bowl, mix the yogurt, raw honey, saffron, and

turmeric until all ingredients are fully incorporated and the mixture has a golden, glowing hue.

Apply the mask with a brush or your middle and ring fingers with light pressure to clean the skin. Let the mask sit for 10 minutes, and then rinse with warm water.

Finish the treatment with a few splashes of cool water, then apply a light moisturizer.

Sunbath Therapy

As a child, I lived for summer days outdoors; any day in the sunshine was a good day to me. Once I was old enough to decide where I'd travel to and where I'd like to live, the sunshine became a factor in my plans. I love exploring deserts and remote island beaches, sun high overhead illuminating the day.

Natural light helps to regulate the circadian rhythm, the natural clock that supports the body in carrying out day-to-day functions. This rhythm regulates our serotonin and melatonin production; serotonin is found throughout the body, giving us feelings of well-being, and melatonin is released by the pineal gland in the brain, regulating the sleep and wake cycle. When we take in healthy amounts of sunlight, these hormones find a state of stasis.

Most of us know that too much sun exposure can be damaging; however, a daily practice of small amounts of exposure to sunlight has myriad benefits. Studies have shown that exposure to this natural source of fire has psychological benefits—uplifting our mood and creating a sense of focus and calm—as well as physical benefits like improved circulation and the release of toxins.

HOW TO DO IT

Find a space outdoors with natural sunlight, avoiding intense direct rays. Choose a time of day when the rays are indirect, shortly after sunrise or close to sunset. The ideal time is before 8 a.m. or after 5 p.m. Wear light-colored natural fiber clothing.

Soak in the sun for up to 20 minutes, ensuring that you're hydrated and paying close attention to how you feel throughout the practice. If the temperature is on the hotter side, drape a cool towel over your face and head. If you find yourself sweating, move into a space with less direct light.

To close the sunbathing therapy session, take a cool shower to rinse the body of toxins released through sweat and bring the body temperature back into equipoise.

GROUND

AFFIRMATION

I transform fear into determination.

The kinetic energy of fire inspires evolution. When there is too much heat in the body, it can manifest as "fiery" emotions like irritability and anger. Whether subtly, like the spark of a match, or with intensity, like the power of a bonfire, these practices support bold, energetic releases of low vibrational emotions.

Candle Gazing

Candle gazing, or *trataka sadhana* ("the spiritual practice of gazing"), is a practice of placing singular focus on a flame to deepen meditation and awaken intuition through strengthening the third eye chakra.

When we fix our gaze on a specific point, we can improve focus and cultivate mindfulness. With an open third eye chakra, we connect more deeply with our inner knowing and sense of awareness.

The only tool needed for this practice is a candle. Choose your candle thoughtfully—consider natural ingredients, like soy or beeswax, and essential oil aromas.

HOW TO DO IT

Set up a quiet space, where lights can be dimmed and you can focus uninterrupted. To elevate the experience, set your space with crystals, herbs, or other special objects.

Light your candle.

Find a comfortable seat and begin by breathing quietly for several minutes while gazing into the candle flame. Imagine releasing lower vibrational thoughts and energies.

Envision the new feelings, emotions, and energy that you would like to call into your life.

Sit in meditation for 3 minutes, building up to 30 minutes.

To close the meditation, blow out the candle and give thanks to the energy of the fire, and yourself.

Fire-Releasing Ritual

I've been leading retreats, workshops, and moon circles for years, and the fire-releasing ritual is a practice I include in just about every experience. In my travels, while working with wisdom keepers in the South Pacific, Central America, Mexico, the Caribbean, the American Southwest, and my hometown of New Orleans, the fire-releasing ritual is a potent practice for letting go.

Fire-releasing rituals have been practiced over time by various cultures and communities, and almost all focus on detoxifying and revitalizing via the forces of nature. The symbolic essence of the fire-releasing ritual is to release old habits and let go of old stories, inner turmoil, and drama. Through this release comes rebirth, transformation, and renewal. The fire-releasing ritual supports us in harnessing kinetic energy and then using it to create powerful shifts in our lives.

HOW TO DO IT

Gather several candles, a lighter or matches, a small bowl of water, a journal and writing implement, and scraps of paper (keep the slips of paper small so as not to cause overwhelming smoke).

Light your candles in a circle around you, representing the sun. If you have only one candle, that's okay too. Spend a moment focusing on the candle flames, inviting your persistent thoughts to dissipate.

Bring awareness to what you'd like to invite into your life. Take a moment to call to mind an image of yourself living this invitation. In my practice, I include a moment of journaling, reflecting on what energy I'd like to cultivate more of in my life. Write this statement by beginning with the phrase "I am inviting." For example: *I am inviting peace into my relationships and joyful creative expression into my career.*

Next, honor ancestors who've created a path for you to thrive; return to your journal and write an "I am honoring" statement. For example: *I am honoring _____, who has gone before me, creating a path for my journey.*

Reflect on what is no longer serving you. This could be in your physical body, in your emotions, or in your mind. Once you've considered those thoughts, write each one on a slip of paper.

After you've written your notes, touch each paper to a candle flame to set it alight. As the paper flames, let each thought burn away and purify from your subconscious mind. (Be careful not to let the paper burn too long—no burned fingers.)

Drop the lit paper into the bowl of water. As the fire and paper hit the water and the water extinguishes the flame, consider that old idea or belief purified from your mind— you've burned it and washed it away.

Repeat these steps until your mind is clear and your heart is at ease.

Honor Your Sacred Rage

This practice was initially shared with me by an astrologer friend and *Oui, We* contributing writer Chelsea Jewel as we discussed our fire sign placements in our natal charts. Our charts are so much more than our sun and moon sign—exploring your chart to get an understanding of where you may naturally have more fiery feelings, for example, can help you move through challenging emotions when they arise. When we're experiencing the energies of fire in our emotional body, it can manifest as intense feelings of frustration and resentment at one end of the spectrum, and as rage at the other end.

What angers and triggers you is meant to show you what you're most passionate about, so you're moved to take heart-centered action.

HOW TO DO IT

Designate a safe time and space for you to fully reflect on and feel the challenging emotions. Then, explore high-intensity activities that allow you to acknowledge and move through them, such as taking a kickboxing class and setting an intention to channel your feelings as you kick and punch your way through class. A few other ideas: visit an ax-throwing studio, scream while listening to heavy rock music in your car, or take it out on the weeds growing in your backyard.

Using your body to process emotions is key to honoring your inner fire.

When you can accept and release emotions this way, you'll likely come out on the other side with renewed clarity, inspiration, and motivation to move forward.

NOURISH

AFFIRMATION

I honor my own divinity.
I attract well-being into my life.

Fire keeps us warm; it's the resource we need to prepare our meals and gives us the regenerative fuel to keep our bodies fit. Warm your body from the inside—and stay cozy—with warming spices and a tea ritual, or visit a sauna or hot yoga studio for a full-body fire glow.

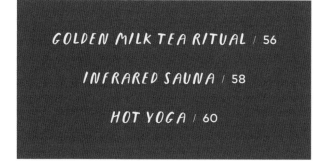

Golden Milk Tea Ritual

You know a fire ingredient is present in a recipe before you even taste it. Think of the deep aromas of ingredients like ginger, allspice, cardamom, and cloves. Then there are pungent spices like chili, cayenne, coriander, cumin, and turmeric. Foods like tomatoes, mangoes, oranges, garlic, and peppers have a warming effect on the body as well.

In all my years of exploring tonics, tinctures, and healing beverages, this particular beverage, golden milk, an Ayurvedic delight, has always been my favorite. It's perfect any time of day and has so many soothing benefits. Golden milk's warming spices aid digestion and circulation, and turmeric reduces inflammation. It's also known to increase your immunity, filter toxins from your blood, and brighten your complexion from the inside.

HOW TO MAKE IT

½ cup fresh dairy or nondairy milk
½ tsp turmeric paste (see Note)
¼ in piece unpeeled ginger, thinly sliced
1 Tbsp honey
1 Tbsp coconut oil
Ground cinnamon or cayenne pepper

In a small saucepan over medium heat, whisk the milk, turmeric paste, ginger, honey, and coconut oil with ½ cup filtered water until it boils.

Turn the heat to low and simmer for about 10 minutes, allowing the flavors to combine. Blowing first to cool it, sip a small spoonful to taste, and add more spices if desired.

Strain through a fine-mesh sieve into a mug and top with a dash of cinnamon or cayenne, as you prefer.

NOTE: Turmeric paste is a mixture of ¼ cup dried turmeric, ½ tsp black pepper, and ½ cup filtered water, heated to combine and then stored in the refrigerator in a glass jar. It can be used in all sorts of dishes: I like to add it to gluten-free pasta in the evening and to eggs for weekend brunch.

Infrared Sauna

There's so much value in visiting an infrared sauna: to detox, sleep better, and improve circulation without the potential damage of direct sun rays. There was a time when the only way to enjoy a visit to the sauna was by either traveling to a spa or having a gym membership. Today there are many more accessible ways to get these benefits.

Ranging from 10 minutes to an hour, each sauna session gives us a moment of quiet to catch up on reading, meditation, or simply introspective time to tune in to our inner voice. Sauna treatment is also especially nice for someone intensifying their daily workout, as it can work miracles on sore muscles.

HOW TO DO IT

Before your trip to the sauna, make sure you're completely hydrated, and be prepared to sweat.

Ideally, enjoy your sauna session in the buff; if that's not possible, drape a towel over yourself or wear a bathing suit, or at most loose, lightweight clothing. If you don't have a sauna near you, there's also the at-home option of a sauna blanket. Be sure to read the instructions for your blanket, and follow the guidelines for the appropriate amount of time and what to wear to ensure you're not overheating.

Once your session is complete, allow your body plenty of time to cool down. When you feel ready, take a bath or a shower, and continue to drink plenty of water to stay hydrated and balanced.

Hot Yoga

Hot yoga was the first yoga practice that inspired my interest in becoming a certified yoga teacher. I began practicing when I'd just moved to a new city and immediately was hooked. My body awakened as I stretched in the heated air. The asanas seemed to flow in a new way as the warmth moved through me. I connected with awareness to my breath, inhaling and exhaling, finding a perfect balance of airflow.

Yogis know that while regular practice will support your strength and flexibility, the physical part is just one component of what it's all about. Yoga is a mental and spiritual practice, and to truly feel that connection, I love practicing in an environment that emulates nature.

When I begin my hot yoga practice, I imagine being on the seaside on a warm summer day, with Mama Earth guiding me through the movements. Of course, most hot yoga classes don't take place on the beach in the sunshine; however, the temperature in the room may lead you to find yourself there in your mind.

Yoga invites you to explore your vibrancy. It's a practice of self-compassion, gifting us harmony in our bodies, our lives, and our relationships. It's an unlearning, a generating, a reorganizing, a bliss-inducing practice that encourages us to find more joy in our lives.

Hot yoga typically takes place in a heated room, with the temperature reaching up to 105 degrees Fahrenheit. The traditional hot yoga practice is composed of twenty-six postures plus two breathing exercises; before beginning a hot yoga practice, hydrate and wear clothing that you feel comfortable moving and sweating in. It's always wise to talk with the yoga teacher before class to learn more about the practice offered at your studio. I've found hot yoga to be incredibly wonderful for muscle tightness, overall flexibility, confidence, and perseverance. If you can make your way through the twenty-six hot yoga postures, you can do almost anything!

After your hot yoga class, spend some time in quiet reflection or writing in your journal. Here are a few prompts to guide you:

When I move my body, I find I'm able to release . . .

There's a flame within my soul. When it's burning brightly, I notice that I am . . .

Stepping outside of my comfort zone gives me the courage to . . .

I FIND GROUNDING IN CREATION.
I JOURNEY INTO THE DEPTHS OF MY
EMOTIONS AND SENSUALITY WITH EASE.

Earth is our grounding force. The earth is our bedrock: the soil and pebbles underfoot as we hike its hills and climb its mountains, the nurturing foundation of trees, and all other plant life. Earth-aligned wellness practices are designed to be slow and steady as we build our foundation.

Earth is associated with rootedness—it invokes practicality, balance, and sensibility. It's the element related to material goods, stability, and security. The earth element is deeply connected to the cyclic rhythm and patterns of nature and the electromagnetic energy of our planet, and it rules the cycles of life: new beginnings and endings, death and rebirth, as life comes from the fertility of the earth and then returns to the ground, decomposing and beginning the cycle again.

People with a higher concentration of earth energy are loyal, steadfast, dedicated, and determined. They enjoy routine and a structured approach to day-to-day living. There's also a sensual and physical embodiment of vitality in earth energy; they're purveyors and collectors of beautiful, worldly things. They find glory in the natural environment.

When we're aligned with the earth's energies, we feel tenacious, nourished, and poised. On the other hand, when we're experiencing the shadow side of Earth, we may notice feelings of materialism, stubbornness, and immobility.

Align more deeply to the earth's energy through whole-some food, experiences, and activities like cooking classes, farmers' market visits, and agritourism. Explore forests, farms, and fields, and visit places offering a deep sense of rest and reconnection.

THE EARTH ELEMENT

ARCHETYPE

Farmer, Builder, Craftsman

SEASON

Winter

Winter, the season of surrender in which the earth lies cold, exemplifies nature's deep stillness. Like animals, we're invited to hibernate, directing our energy inward to consider our own metamorphosis to come.

LUNAR PHASE

Waning Moon

The waning moon follows the full moon—as the light starts to retreat, it's a time to express gratitude and reap the benefits of your work. Use this time to release stagnant energy, celebrate completion, and cultivate rest.

CELESTIAL BODY

Venus

Venus is named after the Roman goddess of love, pleasure, and beauty. It was given its moniker by ancient astronomers who were awed by the mystique and glamour of the brightest planet visible to the human eye. Venus governs our aesthetic vision, creative expression, and romantic relationships.

DIRECTION

North

Earth is the element of the north, represented by the dirt beneath us, the connection to our physical self, and the tangible world around us. The north calls us to seek balance and a sense of direction for the future. Earth energy is most present at midnight—the zenith of nighttime darkness, when we're furthest from daylight hours.

ASTROLOGICAL SIGNS

Capricorn, Taurus, Virgo

Practical and reliable earth signs make for the most pragmatic friends and colleagues. While they're organized and unwavering, they're also quite epicurean and sensual to the core. They recognize beauty, artistry, and craftsmanship, and they have a high sensibility for quality.

SENSE

Smell

The earth element is related to the sense of smell. We take in all of the earth's bounty via our nose. Imagine cut grass, moist soil after a rain, moss on rocks, gathered pinecones, flower blossoms, or eucalyptus trees.

NATURE TOOL KIT

ANYTHING INVOKING SENSUALITY, ROMANCE, AND A SENSE OF GROUNDING

BONE

PERIDOT

HONEY

TOURMALINE

HIMALAYAN SALT

DRIED HERBS

TURQUOISE

LICORICE ROOT

HEMATITE, CEDARWOOD, VETIVER, AND PATCHOULI ESSENTIAL OILS

LAVA STONE

GLOW

AFFIRMATION

I find stillness in my breath.
I'm at home in my body.

We're so fortunate to enjoy the cornucopia of earthly delights available on this planet. But we sometimes experience the vices of worldly materialism, self-doubt, and envy. The rituals in this section feature simple, natural ingredients designed to support your inner and outer illumination and ancient practices to leave you naturally radiant.

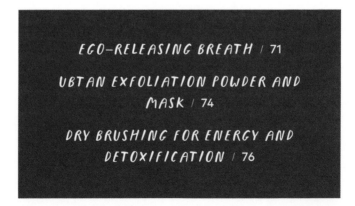

Ego-Releasing Breath

First, let's talk about the ego. It can get a bad rap. Its number one job—what it's purely designed to do—is to keep us safe. The ego supports basic survival; it is an inner voice that limits us. The ego lives in the past and future, constantly analyzing what's happened before and considering what might happen next. It can be controlling, encourage fear, and create resistance.

There is, of course, a time and a place for this. For example, should we be on a desert hike, all alone, in a remote area, the ego can keep us from being eaten by a mountain lion; in a less extreme example, it can heighten our senses when walking home late at night.

On the other hand, there are many times when the ego keeps us in our comfort zone, and as many wise folks have said, transformation and possibility are on the other side of comfort. Many yoga practices work by encouraging us to go beyond what we're accustomed to feeling. As we begin to make peace with discomfort, the ego relinquishes control and allows us to listen to the voice of intuition.

Intuition sits on the opposite end of the spectrum to ego; it is rooted in kindness and love for self. It's an inner voice that guides us toward positive actions, the greatest good, and brave momentum.

When I trained to become a certified kundalini yoga instructor, I found the concept of Ten Body energetic anatomy to be quite enlightening and especially relevant when learning to work with the ego and intuition. Yoga practitioners know that the Western approach to anatomy tends to leave something out. One of the ways we can understand our aura, our mindset, and our vitality is to learn about and engage our ten bodies. In the Ten Body system, we have three mental bodies and six energy bodies in addition to our single physical body.

Before we begin the ego-releasing breath practice, it's helpful to understand this system and how each of our "bodies" works together with the rest. Here's a quick overview of all ten bodies:

SOUL BODY—Our flow of spirit and connection to infinite consciousness

THE NEGATIVE MIND—The assessment of protection while balancing discipline and integrity

THE POSITIVE MIND—Our playfulness, optimism, and self-worth

THE NEUTRAL MIND—Our ability to recognize polarity, see duality, and create balance

THE PHYSICAL BODY—Our human vessel holding the energy of the teacher within and serving as an anchor for the other nine bodies

THE ARC LINE—Our halo, connection to our intuition, and the nucleus of our aura

THE AURA—The electromagnetic field of energy that surrounds our Physical Body and holds our life force energy

THE PRANIC BODY—Associated with the breath, our energetic ability to take inspired action

THE SUBTLE BODY—Our ability to live beyond human form, our capacity for mastery

THE RADIANT BODY—Our charisma and magnetism, our inner glow

The ego-releasing breath creates a powerful tenth body, our Radiant Body, encouraging courage, nobility, charisma, and magnetism. When our Radiant Body is vital and our Arc Line clear, our presence communicates contentment, containment, completeness, and consciousness. When it is unwell and cloudy, we may look outward for security versus trusting what's within, as we listen to the ego rather than our intuition.

This simple but effective exercise has fantastic benefits. Energetically, it strengthens and cleanses the lungs and opens the heart, plus it balances the hemispheres of the brain to guide us into mental clarity while quieting the egoic mind.

POSTURE: Raise your arms over your head in a V shape. Flex your fingers, then bend them at the middle knuckle so the pads of your fingertips rest at the top of your palms. Point your thumbs toward the sky. The thumbs represent the ego and our experience here on Earth; with your thumbs pointing upward, you plug into the higher realms, going above your earthly thoughts, and with arms spread in a V, you funnel in a new way of thinking.

GAZE: Close your eyes and focus on your third eye center. (Learn more about activating the third eye on page 170.)

BREATH: There are options for breathing based on what feels best to you. You can breathe with a long deep breath, inhaling and exhaling through your nose to create a sense of powerful calm. Try incorporating Breath of Fire breathing (page 45) into this practice for a more intense experience.

Start with 3 minutes of the ego-releasing breath and continue to build your practice up to 30 minutes.

Ubtan Exfoliation Powder and Mask

The traditional Ayurvedic skin and body care regimen includes daily cleansing with ubtans, traditional herbal powders. These are blended to cleanse, tone, and moisturize the skin while delivering essential nutrients. Daily application of ubtan can also support the lymphatic system and is known to tone muscles while improving circulation.

Your ubtan powder can serve as an all-in-one daily body cleanser and exfoliant, regardless of your skin type. In addition, ubtan face masks will leave you with extraordinarily fresh and hydrated skin, clearing your dermis of congestion; it's extra effective for oily or blemish-prone skin.

There are quite a few recipes for creating your own ubtan powder mask; this is a blend that I enjoy using. The flour and powder combination helps facilitate smoothing, and milk helps to minimize discoloration, leaving the skin glowing and with fewer visible spots. You may want to experiment with a variety of recipes, including ingredients like rose water, lemon, turmeric, or aloe vera, to find the perfect blend for you.

HOW TO MAKE AND USE IT

Start by adding a ½ cup of chickpea or almond flour base to a small bowl. Add 1 Tbsp of sandalwood powder, which helps to alleviate flakiness and is said to have antibacterial properties. If your skin tends to be extra oily, add up to an additional 1 Tbsp of milk powder. If you're experiencing a breakout, add 1 tsp of turmeric powder.

Whisk together the dry ingredients—the ubtan—and then, in equal parts to the powder, add water with a squeeze of lemon (for oilier skin) or milk or yogurt (for combination skin) and combine until you have created an even paste. For dry or sensitive skin, you can also add a quarter-sized amount of aloe vera to the final mixture.

TO USE AS A DAILY CLEANSER: Apply the mixture evenly to your face with your fingers, then wash and dry your hands. Let the mixture dry for 30 to 45 seconds, and then with dry fingers, gently stroke your face in an upward circular motion. Some of the mixture will fall from your face, so place a towel on your lap or bend over your sink as you cleanse and exfoliate.

TO USE AS A MASK: Apply the mixture evenly to your face, wash and dry your hands as before, and then lie down for 10 minutes.

Rinse the mixture and finish with a moisturizer of your choice.

Dry Brushing for Energy and Detoxification

As our largest organ, our skin plays a critical role in our overall health and well-being. It's responsible for protecting our inner organs, operating as part of our immune system, and supporting our ability to release toxins. Dry brushing is my go-to for reducing puffiness, improving skin elasticity, lifting and toning, and enhancing my natural glow.

We completely shed and renew our skin around every twenty-eight days; interestingly, that's the same length of time as a moon cycle. So the skin you looked at in the mirror this morning will be wholly replaced a month from today. You can help clear your dead surface skin cells and keep your skin looking bright and renewed by exfoliating it regularly.

To do this, you can use the ubtan powder you made in the previous exercise (page 75); dry brushing is another wonderful option. Skin brushing originated in India over five millennia ago as a tenet of Ayurveda. It can be traced back to most ancient civilizations as a prebathing ritual to support oxygenating the skin, which increases cell turnover and stimulates circulation.

Dry brushing will clear your pore openings on the exterior and leave your skin looking bright, energized, and supple. Internally, it improves circulation at the skin's surface, stimulating the lymphatic system, and speeding up the process of eliminating metabolic waste from the body. Dry brushing is known to reduce the appearance of cellulite as it breaks up and softens fatty tissue beneath the skin. As the bristles pass over your skin, you'll notice an invigorating stimulation of your nervous system.

HOW TO DO IT

Get a firm-bristle brush for all-over body brushing and a softer brush if you intend to brush your face as well.

Before your morning shower, take a few minutes to brush your entire body and face. Start at your feet, working up toward your torso, using long even strokes in the direction of your heart. Maintain a firm, consistent pressure, stroking each area of your body with the brush three to six times, depending on your level of sensitivity.

Finish with your facial brush, working in an upward circular motion starting at your neck and working up to your forehead.

Once you've completed the process, finish with a shower and then a moisturizer or body oil.

GROUND

AFFIRMATION

I'm anchored to the earth and
integrate all that I've gathered. I am a reflection
of Mother Nature's magic.

Stand outside in the grass barefoot, take a walk in a local
greenspace, go hiking or camping, try forest bathing, and
let go of the earthly possessions that weigh you down.
These rituals will anchor you and strengthen the connection
to your body, your health, and healing.

Earthing

As a child, I loved going out in the early-summer evenings, shoeless, my feet racing across wet grass sparkling with evening dew as my sister and I chased fireflies. I didn't know then what I know now: The practice of bare feet to grass is a natural way to reset the circadian rhythm. My sister and I would sleep like babies. Now it's one of my favorite ways to find a little evening bliss.

Traditionally, the rhythms of the day were completely governed by the seasons and the cycles. Today many of us are more connected to technology than we are to the earth. This simple practice—walking barefoot outside, allowing ourselves to be in deep connection with the frequency of the earth—has an array of benefits.

The earth emanates electromagnetic energies, called Schumann resonance frequencies, that support brain function. They are significant because they induce brain states that help us relax, heal, and perceive and experience earth energies.

Earth's energy travels up from the terrestrial surface. When we connect to the earth's natural energy, walking barefoot—whether on grass, sand, dirt, or rock—can diminish chronic pain, fatigue, and other ailments plaguing many people today.

HOW IT WORKS

When our bare skin connects to the earth, free electrons move up into our bodies. These electrons are one of nature's incredible sources of antioxidants, helping to neutralize free radical damage that can cause inflammation and disease.

The earth's energy upgrades our physiology by allowing the body to repair and regenerate, promoting a healthier overall system, vitality, and better sleep. It also harmonizes and stabilizes the body's primary biological rhythms.

Enjoying a meditative walk can further connect you to this grounding practice. Walking meditation is simple and can be done anywhere. Go outside. Walk mindfully, being aware of each step and each breath. Notice the colors, textures, and shapes around you. Hear the sounds, feel the air. Choose an affirmation, focus on it, and when thoughts arise, see them as if they're on a conveyor belt. Let them move past you as you continue to focus on your steps, breath, and surroundings.

If you live in a city environment where finding a natural connection to the earth isn't as easy, there are all sorts of products, including sheets, blankets, sleep mats, pillows, and socks, that are available to support your earthing practice from home.

Create Sacred Space

The Japanese have a custom called ōsōji, or "big clean," according to Marie Kondo of the KonMari Method. The method encourages living among items you genuinely cherish.

The big clean is done with a spirit of gratitude when families gather together for a tidying festival. Ōsōji takes place in December, before the Gregorian calendar begins a new year; in other traditions, spring is the perfect season for refreshing the home.

I personally love to take time each new moon to create sacred space to reimagine and cast a vision for my ideal lifestyle, comb through my earthly objects, and let go of what isn't lighting me up with delight. To create sacred space, consider what it would feel like to live in a state of magic, and imagine how each area of your home would look and feel in that state.

HOW IT WORKS

Start with a spatial detox. Tidy up any clutter, get the junk out of the way, make decisions of what to keep with confidence, choose to hold on to what you truly cherish, and then release what no longer serves your highest good.

The vacuum law of prosperity explains that when you make space for the good, that's when the things you want will begin to manifest. Space allows for movement; when space is filled, the fresh stuff you most desire can't make its way in. By reducing the unnecessary things in your life, you can create the time, atmosphere, and opportunity for what you are manifesting to show up.

For example, if your wallet is full of dry-cleaning receipts and old business cards, clean it out to attract more money. Is your desk piled high with clutter that you never seem to get through? To attract more fulfilling work, reduce the piles to allow for new projects to show up.

To close your ōsōji practice, cleanse the space's energy with smoke (choosing sustainable herbal blends or woods like rosemary or copal).

When you begin your sacred space practice, start with areas where you meditate, journal, bathe, make out, or rest. This may take several days. Crank up your favorite playlist, and work in 10-minute intervals to keep this feeling easy. Take it day by day.

Forest Bathing

One of the most earthly practices available to us is the simple act of spending time deep in nature, slowing down, and immersing ourselves in the essence of the outdoors.

Shinrin-yoku, or "forest bathing," means taking in the atmosphere and experience of the forest while enjoying a leisurely walk among the trees. Shinrin-yoku is a highly regarded practice for healing in Japanese medicine; it's said that spending time among trees creates calming neuropsy-chological effects through changes in the nervous system, reducing the stress hormone cortisol, and boosting the immune system.

There are over sixty shinrin-yoku forests in Japan certified by the Forest Therapy Society. While you may not have a flight booked to Japan soon, there are ways you can replicate the experience at home. If you do choose to visit one of the certified forests, called "forest therapy bases" and "therapy roads," you'll find they're well lit, with gentle slopes; these completely barrier-free environments are fully wheelchair accessible.

Growing up, I lived in an area with a small forest behind my house. It seemed much more significant to me as a child than it likely was; however, I can vividly recall standing in the woods and feeling incredibly free and connected to the power of nature.

The simple goal of this practice is to invite nature in through all five senses, to feel the subtle energy of the forest completely.

HOW TO DO IT

To try forest bathing in your local environment, start by finding a park or forest in your home community. Once you arrive, pack your phone away. If you'd like to keep it with you for safety, that's absolutely fine; however, place it somewhere where you won't have the urge to use it unless in an emergency.

Next, simply walk and breathe. Enjoy the feeling of sunlight on your skin; notice the sound of the leaves beneath your feet and the rustling of the wind in the trees.

Acknowledge the myriad colors of the trees; take in the aroma of the damp moss or the blooms of the local flora. Note the light and shadows, the temperature of the air, the sensations of the season, and the beauty of the landscape.

Pause from time to time to gaze down the path ahead, paying attention to the fine details along the way. Then take a few moments to rest, tuning in deeply to the environment. If you're forest bathing with others, make a commitment to walk in silence until the end.

Once you've completed the journey, share your experiences and celebrate your newly found sense of serenity.

If you don't have time to go outdoors, try bringing the forest into your home self-care experience by using essential oils like hinoki, Aomori Hiba, and cedar in your bath or shower.

NOURISH

AFFIRMATION

I practice conscious eating and slow living,
treating my body as a temple.

These rituals are simple, earthly acts of nourishment. Make
a warm beverage from seeds and foraged flowers, replenish
with a scrub and body oil self-massage treatment after a
long day, or cultivate a garden to keep herbs on hand for
your meals.

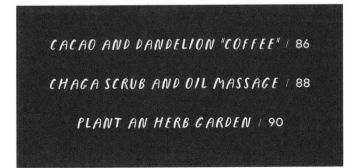

Cacao and Dandelion "Coffee"

I started drinking coffee at a really young age. Not because Starbucks is in every neighborhood, but because my dad worked in France during my childhood. I had these visions of what it must be like to stroll the streets of Paris, ducking into an adorable café, having a coffee and baguette in the morning, and an espresso in the evening after dinner. I had a vision of living a chichi French lifestyle. Coffee transported me to some other world. Hey, my blog is called *Oui, We* because my first trip to Paris inspired me to open up to a different sort of life experience and travel.

Despite my deep love for coffee, I decided a few years ago to give it up to support my health. I started by transitioning to decaf, and when I found a beverage I loved as much as I loved coffee, I gave it up all the way.

My replacement beverage is a blend of cacao and roasted dandelion; it tastes similar to an unsweetened mocha. It uses coconut milk, which is creamy like dairy and rich in fatty and lauric acids, which are lovely for the skin, hair, teeth, and bones. It also has electrolytes that support blood pH and cellular fluid balance.

Cacao is a superfood full of flavonoids, rich in antioxidants that can support the body in warding off everyday toxins. It's also one of the best plant-based sources of calcium, potassium, magnesium, and iron. Dandelion has long been used in herbal medicine to aid digestion and detoxification. My blend also includes chicory and ashwagandha. Chicory powder contains beneficial plant phenols, selenium, manganese, potassium, and vitamins B and C. Ashwagandha is used as a general tonic to boost energy and reduce stress and anxiety. Occasionally I'll add a few rose petals for garnish.

You don't have to give up coffee to enjoy this beverage, but if that's something you're considering, this drink could be your coffee replacement too. This magical beverage offers a moment of blissful indulgence to start or end the day.

HOW TO MAKE IT

¾ cup coconut milk
½ Tbsp cacao powder
½ Tbsp roasted dandelion powder
½ Tbsp roasted chicory powder
1 tsp ashwagandha powder
¼ cup hot filtered water
Crushed cacao nibs for garnish
Rose petals for garnish (optional)
½ tsp honey (optional)

Heat the coconut milk in a small saucepan and allow the milk to simmer.

In a bowl or mug, whisk together the cacao, roasted dandelion, roasted chicory, and ashwagandha powders with the hot water until thoroughly blended.

Slowly incorporate the warmed milk into the mixture and stir until well blended, smooth, and creamy. Add the cacao nibs, and the rose petals and honey (if using).

Chaga Scrub and Oil Massage

Chaga is the king of the medicinal mushrooms—it's a fascinating fungus that has more antioxidant content than blueberries. Chaga supports the skin for graceful aging, healing sun damage, broken capillaries, and hyperpigmentation, making this DIY scrub the perfect superfood for your skin.

Once you've used the scrub to exfoliate, it's time to move into a self-massage. As a traditional Ayurvedic practice and used in tantric traditions, self-massage is incredibly good for you and feels so nurturing and replenishing. In Ayurveda, self-massage using plant-derived oils is known as abhyanga, a traditional form of self-care for people of all ages. A daily abhyanga practice restores balance and enhances well-being and longevity.

The Sanskrit word *sneha* translates as both "oil" and "love," and it's believed that as we saturate our body with oil, abhyanga provides a feeling of being drenched in love. With regular practice, you'll begin to notice toned, glowing skin, improved circulation, and detoxification as you stimulate the lymphatic system.

NOTE: Make sure to source sustainably harvested chaga powder. A lovely benefit: While here we use chaga powder to make a scrub, you can also stir a ½ tsp or so into your daily coffee or smoothie for an antioxidant boost.

> 1 cup water
> 1 Tbsp chaga powder (see Note)
> 2 Tbsp coconut oil
> ¼ cup almond, jojoba, coconut, or safflower oil,
>   depending on preference

Bring the water to a boil in a saucepan. Transfer the water to a bowl, then mix in the powder. Allow the mixture to cool completely.

Stir in the 2 Tbsp of coconut oil.

Apply to clean skin and scrub with an upward motion. Let the mixture sit for 10 minutes, then rinse the areas you've scrubbed. Dry completely.

Warm the ¼ cup of oil slightly, testing to ensure the temperature isn't too hot. Using oil as needed, begin massaging your feet and legs first and work up to your scalp, then back down. Work on each body area with long circular strokes, focusing on even the smallest areas like earlobes and fingers. There is no wrong way to practice self-massage.

Once you've finished, allow the oil to absorb completely into your skin for 10 minutes or so, and then finish with a light warm water rinse.

Plant an Herb Garden

If you've ever opened the refrigerator to grab rosemary, basil, or cilantro for a recipe only to find a pile of plastic containers with dried-out, spoiled herbs, it's time to DIY your own herb garden. Herbs can be used in so many ways and offer many benefits: Basil has antibacterial properties, oregano is an antifungal, and both support the immune system. Parsley and thyme help with indigestion, and cilantro protects against oxidative stress. You can use sage for insect bites and dill for calming the hiccups.

You can also grow medicinal herbs like calendula, lemon balm, holy basil, astragalus, and echinacea. These herbs offer benefits like nerve nourishment, pain relief, and immune support.

In honor of Mother Earth, your health, and diversifying your cuisine, instead of buying herbs and letting them shrivel up in the back of your refrigerator, try planting a kitchen herb garden with these simple supplies.

HOW TO DO IT

Mason jars
Organic potting soil
A handful of foraged rocks for each jar
¼ cup sand for each jar
Seed packets
Labels

Gather your supplies. When choosing your herbs, think about what you already like to eat and which herbs you tend to use the most. Label each jar with the herb name.

Fill each Mason jar, starting with rocks at the bottom, then the sand, and then potting soil to a level about three quarters of the way full.

Sprinkle in a couple of seeds and cover them with additional soil. Pour in a bit of water, just enough to dampen the soil.

Place the jars on a sunny windowsill.

Now be patient and wait for your seedlings to grow. Keep them close to sunlight and give them a small drink every day, being mindful not to overwater. Depending on germinating time, your herbs will sprout when they're ready.

I AM A REFLECTION OF MY DREAMS.
I SEE MY OWN DEPTH IN THE WATERS
OF THE OCEAN, RIVERS, AND LAKES.

Water is nature's element of emotion. Water corresponds to our feelings (we cry when we need to release), our power (consider the strength of a thunderstorm or a tidal wave, and how we sweat after a hard workout), our sense of calm (imagine the serenity of a lake), and our inherent need to nourish (just like plants, we need water to grow and live).

In the spiritual sense, water is our depth, lunar nature, and an expression of our sensitivity and mystery. At the level of individual consciousness, water informs how we cleanse, refresh, and nourish.

Those with a higher concentration of water in their energetic constitution feel things at the soul level. They take family and a sense of home to heart and can be expressive and loving with those in their inner circle. They have a strong intuition and can pick up on the emotions of others easily—sometimes being considered empathic by nature.

When we align with the water energies, we may notice feelings of care, nostalgia, resourcefulness, creativity, and dreaminess. Conversely, when experiencing the shadow side of water, we may notice feelings of caution, sadness, and heartache.

Think of the variety of ways water exists in nature. Consider the rapids of a mighty river or a trickling stream, the waves of the ocean, a frozen lake, or gentle rain. Like its natural expressions, water relates to our flow and how we over-come obstacles.

If you want to bring out your water energy, explore loca-tions that allow for joyous and nourishing activities: rent a boat and spend a day on the water, visit your local farmers' markets and focus on fresh foods or seaside fare, or try a fresh juice each day as your morning beverage.

THE WATER ELEMENT

ARCHETYPE

Mother, Apothecary, Artist

SEASON

Spring

Spring is the season of water. The spring equinox brings rebirth, new growth, and aliveness. Snow melts, and crisp, cool water flows from the mountains into the rivers and streams. Life grows in its wake. Water is the source of all life and the container of prana—the breath that sustains us. Just as the water becomes abundant in nature during this time, the water element in our bodies naturally increases too.

LUNAR PHASE

New Moon

Considered the best time to set intentions, the new moon signals a time to germinate. Traditionally, agricultural societies have used the moon's phases to guide seed planting; the *Farmers' Almanac* even encourages farmers today to use this method. The new moon is the optimal time to allow new ideas to arise, tap into creative flow, and nourish and create routines of self-care.

CELESTIAL BODY

The Moon

The moon represents the divine mother in each of us. It reflects our deepest wishes, our individual mystery, our emotion, and our unconscious. The moon represents how you see yourself: Imagine catching your reflection in a pool of water and taking in both what's on the surface and what lies beneath. Lunar energy is cleansing, cooling, receptive, calming, sensitive, and empathic.

DIRECTION

West

The west draws us into reflecting on our emotions. It invites self-understanding. When we dam up our feelings, just as when we dam up a river, the pressure builds until it finds an outlet. If you seek to get in touch with your inner life, with your emotions, turn toward the west. Water is represented by the late afternoon, the western point on the clock, around 3 p.m. Physically, during that time of day we begin to experience a shift in our water element, when the kidneys go through a renewal cycle.

ASTROLOGICAL SIGNS

Cancer, Scorpio, Pisces

Two of these signs are represented by creatures of the sea: Cancer by the crab and Pisces by the fish. Scorpio is the fixed water sign, represented by the scorpion. There's one fixed sign for each of the four elements; the water signs are considered to be the most grounded and stable of the zodiac. All three are predisposed to have a depth of emotion, sensitivity, and natural psychic wisdom.

SENSE

Taste

Aristotle wrote that water, in its natural state, is tasteless. However, it serves as a vehicle for flavors. In Ayurveda, taste is known as rasa—the basis of nourishment. *Rasa* means "sap" or "juice," representing the primary waters flowing through our body, hydrating and sustaining our well-being.

NATURE TOOL KIT

POPPY FLOWER, VALERIAN, BASIL, AND CITRUS ESSENTIAL OILS

SHELLS

VERBENA-INFUSED WATER

ANYTHING OCEANIC OR REPRESENTING THE SEA

ITEMS THAT REMIND YOU OF YOUR GRANDMOTHERS OR OTHER FEMALE ANCESTORS

TOURMALINE AND QUARTZ CRYSTALS

GLOW

AFFIRMATION

I'm purified and renewed; my past constraints are
released from my auric field.

Water is used for purification on both physical and energetic
levels. Water is fluid, invokes movement, and can be both soft
and powerful. Water is life-giving. Holy water and baptisms
are examples of how water has been used for thousands of
years to spiritually purify. Water also inspires an inner and
outer shine—through breathing techniques and temperature,
we can improve our glandular and circulatory system flow.

The Moon Breath

Consider how water moves: rushing rapids, the shifting of the tides, sweat beading up on our skin, salty tears rolling down our cheeks. Water is an element deeply connected to life flow, as well as the expanse of our emotions and the immeasurable creativity that lives within us all.

In astrology, there is an interconnectedness between the moon and water. At the most basic level, across many spiritual modalities, customs, and cultures, both represent imagination, emotion, intuition, inner knowing, and the feminine.

Our ocean tides are linked to the moon, as its gravitational pull is exerted on the earth's water, creating bulges that move across the surface and affect currents and shorelines. *Tides: The Science and Spirit of the Ocean*, by Jonathan White, is a wonderful read if you're interested in learning more.

During the waxing gibbous phase, the moon is approaching the full phase, and during the waning crescent phases, the moon is approaching the new phase. During these two times every month, the highs and lows of the tides increase until they reach their maximum intensity. The most extreme high tides, called spring tides, occur when the earth, moon, and sun align, sometimes creating an eclipse. It's a marvelous and magical natural occurrence.

This breath practice inspires us to explore the depths of our creativity and connects us to our own lunar energies.

Our prana, or breath—the vital wind that brings life force into our body—creates unique energies as it moves in and out through the nostrils. The left nostril and right nostril each have different effects corresponding with the qualities associated with each side of the brain.

The nerves going out from the two brain hemispheres cross at the level of the eyebrows. The brain's left hemisphere is connected to the right side of the body and the right nostril, and its right hemisphere connects to the left side of the body and the left nostril.

We have a wide array of techniques to control our moods and energies through the simple mechanism of closing or opening one of the nostrils.

HOW TO DO IT

This breath exercise focuses on the left nostril, the end of the ida nadi—one of the three main channels of energy running through the body according to yogic science. Breathing through the left nostril stimulates the lunar side: creativity, emotions, a sense of flow, and intuition. It also creates a cleansing and cooling sensation.

To practice moon breathing, simply cover your right nostril and breathe long and deeply through the left, in and out. Practice for at least a minute to stimulate the lunar energies. A daily practice of 3 minutes can bring calmness and balance to your day and elevate your energy, vitality, and confidence in your creativity.

DIY Ice Mask

As much as I love creating recipes with plant ingredients and dreaming up skincare concoctions with Ayurvedic herbs and spices, sometimes what we need is the most natural ingredient of all: water. For this mask, all you'll need is a lightweight organic cloth (cotton or linen works perfectly) and ice cubes from your freezer.

When you wake up with puffy skin after a night out with friends or too much popcorn during movie night, an ice pack mask will immediately bring down the swelling. I especially like this ice mask after a long flight—it's a wonderful way to relieve dehydrated and inflamed "airplane skin."

There are ice packs specifically designed for the face, available in beauty supply stores and online; however, many are made with plastics and other toxic ingredients, so making your own ice mask with these simple items you already have at home is the most sustainable approach.

HOW TO DO IT

Begin with clean, moisturized skin. Lay out a lightweight organic facial towel. On top of the towel, arrange ice cubes in a circle the size of your face.

Roll in the edges of the towel to ensure the ice cubes are secured and completely covered by the towel.

Scoop up the towel and place it against your face, making sure the ice cubes remain tucked inside the towel so as not to make direct contact with your skin. Situate the towel so the cubes encircle your whole face.

If you want to get fancy, freeze a couple of cucumber slices and slip them inside the towel, placing them over your closed eyes.

Leave the mask on for 10 to 15 minutes, depending on your sensitivity.

When you finish the practice, for skincare bonus points and to further the depuffing and promote lymphatic drainage, roll your facial skin with a cold jade roller.

The ice mask plus jade roller will increase the blood flow to your face. You may notice a few moments of redness at first, but afterward the effects will be visible—a brighter, depuffed complexion.

Hydrotherapy

Hydrotherapy is a fascinating and potent practice to support the elimination of toxins in the body. The euphoric feeling from an at-home hydrotherapy session is truly as good as anything you'll get at a spa.

With just a few minutes in the shower, you can improve your overall well-being, wake up your body and mind, detoxify, and strengthen your entire nervous system.

In yoga traditions, hydrotherapy is called ishnaan. The hydrotherapy practice uses alternating temperatures, moving from warm to cold, to influence your system. The warm water relaxes the muscles, and the cold water stimulates them. The known benefits of a daily cold shower blast include boosting your immune system by increasing your white blood cell count and clearing toxins as the capillaries open.

The practice is known to improve your stress response and willpower—if you can endure a few minutes of high-intensity cold, you can endure day-to-day challenges and boost your metabolic rate.

The science behind this practice: Cold water stimulates the body in a way that can improve circulation and purify the organs. As cold water hits your body, blood will be pulled from your extremities to your internal organs. As the blood retreats, it flushes the capillary system, giving it a vigorous workout.

Start slowly, adding a short 30-second blast of cold at the end of your regular warm shower. You'll exit the shower with a healthy glow, exhilaration, and an elevated emotional state.

HOW TO DO IT

Before climbing into the shower, start by giving yourself a quick full-body massage with plant-based body oil. Jojoba, coconut, or olive oil are all good choices.

Start the shower with warm water, just as you regularly would when taking your daily shower.

When you're ready to begin the hydrotherapy, get the cold water flowing. Start by exposing your extremities—feet, hands, arms, and legs—to the cold. Move to your face next.

Move in and out of the water several times, letting the cold water flow from your head and face all along your body, constantly massaging your body until you begin to get used to the cooler temperature. Start with 10 seconds in the cold, 10 seconds out, building up to 30 seconds and beyond. (It's generally a good idea to protect the genitals and the lower back/kidney area from long-term cold exposure.)

When you're finished, return the water temperature to hot if you'd like to warm up, then dry off with vigor, starting at your feet, working up your legs, moving upward with the towel to simulate a dry brushing technique to help further stimulate your circulation. I love this practice first thing in the morning to start my day off with a serious glow!

NOTE: Avoid hydrotherapy if you're experiencing a fever, rheumatism, or heart disease, or if you're menstruating or pregnant.

GROUND

AFFIRMATION

Refreshing energy streams forth from
my heart, cleansing and revitalizing my
body and mind.

Water is wonderfully grounding because of how closely it relates to the earth's negative ions. Negative ions help the body heal, detoxify, and promote feelings of contentment. Practice visualization-style meditations and exercises that invite feelings of flow. And work with water infused with lunar energy to cultivate a feeling of balance and connectedness.

Meditation of Creative Flow

This is a rhythmic meditation, connecting to flow and future vision. It's especially powerful when you're feeling stagnant or overwhelmed and need to let go of stressors to tap into your creativity. It involves visualization and the practice of mantra to reset your inner narrative.

You can practice this visualization-style meditation anytime you're feeling burdened or overwhelmed or experiencing intense stressors that you need to process to move forward and feel balanced, grounded, and productive.

HOW TO DO IT

Start with engaging your breath. Inhale and hold your breath comfortably. Then, as you retain the breath, meditate on the number zero. Say to yourself: *All is zero; each thought is zero; my stress is zero; my problems are zero.*

Bring to mind anything creating stress for you, and imagine dialing the energy around that stressor to zero. Even if you don't yet believe it, begin to imagine dialing any swirling thoughts down to zero. Meditate on all negative emotional, mental, and physical conditions and situations. As each thing crosses your mind, bring it to zero.

Once you've released your stressors, imagine you're floating in a body of water: the sea, a lake, or whatever body of water feels best to you. Feel the water rising beneath you, offering support. As you inhale, imagine waves gently rolling in; as you exhale, the waves gently roll away. Let this water hold you. Feel its coolness on your skin, hear its movement as it splashes against your body, smell the salty air. Tell yourself: *Here in this water, my imagination is free, and my creativity is boundless.*

Envision your body floating to the shoreline. Stand up and take a moment to let the water fully cleanse you. Let the water rinse all the way through, cleansing each of your energy centers, beginning at your crown chakra, located at the top of your head and working all the way down to the root chakra, located at the base of your spine.

Note if you're holding on to any pain, tightness, or sadness inside your body. Let the water rinse those feelings away. Notice that an inner shine, a golden light, is coming from within you as you rest on the shoreline. Observe an outer glow as well: the sun creating a ring of light around you. Allow this light to permeate you until your inner light and the outer light have merged into one.

Once you've completed the visualization, close with this mantra: "I am creative infinity." Say the mantra out loud several times, and write it in places you'll see throughout the day too.

Moon Water

By syncing our daily lives to the moon cycle, we align to the wealth of the universe. The moon tells us when to look inward and reflect, when to tap into intentions, when to take action through creative self-expression, when to amplify our manifestation powers, and when to cleanse our energy.

Timing your daily rituals to coincide with the lunar phases is a beautiful way to stay in the flow of life while connecting with the natural elements.

In astrology, the moon is ruled by the sign of Cancer and has an energetic connection to our emotional body. This simple ritual can help you explore your inner sensitivities while providing a moment of care in the process.

You can make moon water during any phase of the moon, but it is most commonly done on a full moon and charged overnight in the moonlight. There are limitless ways you can use your moon water.

HOW TO DO IT

Take a Mason jar with a lid and fill it with water, either filtered or from the tap. Secure the lid. To amplify the water, you can place crystals on the lid; blue calcite, lapis lazuli, labradorite, selenite, and moonstone are all wonderful for tuning into your intuitive flow.

Place the jar and crystals outside or on a windowsill where it will be in the direct line of the moonlight overnight. As you place the jar, spend a few minutes considering your intentions. Look into the zodiac sign of that particular moon phase when setting intentions to best work with the energies of the current cycle. For example, on an Aquarius or Pisces moon, set intentions around intuition, vision, and dreams.

In the morning, collect the jar and use the moon water however you wish! Here are a few ideas of what you can do with it:

DRINK IT—Take a sip or two every day, reminding yourself of your intentions and the power of the moon.

BATHE YOUR CRYSTALS IN IT—Crystals can absorb all types of energy. Bathing them in your moon water will give them a refresh and amplify their power.

BEAUTIFY WITH IT—Place your moon water in a spray bottle, add a few drops of your favorite essential oil, and use it as a facial toner each morning.

Arc Line Clearing

In the yoga tradition, the Arc Line is the nucleus of the aura, the halo, the beaming of our essence—it's the projection of who we are and what people can feel when we walk into a room. Think of a time when you were at a social event, and as someone walked into the room, it was as if everyone could feel their energy. It wasn't that they had the best haircut or most amazing shoes. It was simply that their aura was radiant and magnetic.

In kundalini yoga tradition, the human has ten bodies (see page 72), and the Arc Line is the sixth body. The Arc Line lives in the space encircling your head, around the level of your earlobes. This aureole field of energy holds your karmic story. Some people also have a second Arc Line running nipple to nipple, giving you the enhanced capacity for sensitivity, attraction, and subtle intuition.

This practice, involving breathwork, meditation, movement, and visualization, clears karmic energy and allows you to shine. A daily practice of Arc Line cleansing can leave you feeling refreshed, rejuvenated, and vibrant.

HOW TO DO IT

If you're able to, seat yourself on a cushion on the floor in easy pose, a cross-legged traditional meditation posture. Sit up tall with a straight spine. You can sit in a chair if that's more comfortable. Relax your elbows and extend your forearms straight out in front of your body with your palms slightly cupped, facing up as if they're catching rain. As you begin the practice, imagine you are scooping water while lifting your arms up. Envision yourself cleansing your Arc Line with a flick of your wrists, sending the water up and over your head in one smooth, graceful motion, stretching your hands and arms as far back over your shoulders as you can. Repeat.

As you move, breathe long and deep, inhaling and exhaling through your nose, expanding your belly with each inhale, and releasing your breath, deflating your belly with each exhale.

Continue for 3 minutes.

NOURISH

AFFIRMATION

The force of life flows through me.
I'm nourished from the inside out.

Water is the ultimate healer. Our bodies rely on water
for essential functions: metabolizing, maintaining our
temperature, and electrolyte balance. Snack on citrus fruits
or melons, or stop by your local juice shop when you need a
midday pick-me-up. Enjoy a warming tea ritual for mindfulness and hydration. Consider full-body immersion—a bath
or a swim—for the ultimate nourishment.

Warming Tea Ritual

Teas each have unique properties and effects and can support the body in a variety of ways. They can be made with leaves, herbs, spices, fruits, and other plants and are high in antioxidants, and offer a variety of wellness benefits. The antioxidant flavonoids and natural caffeine of green tea will give you energy and put color in your cheeks; tea brewed with warming ingredients like ginger, cinnamon, or turmeric enhances healing.

Practicing a tea ritual or ceremony allows us to commune with nature by incorporating each element: the water to brew the tea, the fire and air to boil the water, and the earth represented by the plant ingredients that make up the brew.

Years ago, I visited a teahouse called Floating Leaves, owned by a tea practitioner named Shiuwen. Her intention at Floating Leaves is to bring Eastern and Western cultures together in one room. She grew up in Taiwan, where serving tea was simply a part of daily life, a way to bring people together. Shiuwen believes tea gives us an opportunity to understand each other beyond cultural barriers and get past the bounds of the mind, creating a taste of freedom.

Since my experience with Shiuwen, I've made it a regular practice to enjoy a simple tea ritual as often as possible. I enjoy this ritual in my garden in the afternoon, or before bed after a hectic day.

Consider incorporating tea into your life as a substitute for coffee occasionally. It won't stress the adrenals and can help stabilize your blood sugar. For a memorable experience, consider the social aspect of tea: Invite friends over to share a big pot of tea rather than cocktails. It's a wonderful way to enjoy time with people you love while supporting your health and hydration—plus, there's no hangover to contend with the next day!

Before you begin, be sure to stock your kitchen with various sustainably sourced, fair-trade teas. With a kettle, an infuser, and your teacup and/or a teapot, you're ready to begin.

HOW TO DO IT

Sit comfortably in your space and ground yourself, taking a few deep breaths. Then turn your awareness inward and listen to your body to see what it needs. Allow this to guide your tea choice.

Put your tea into a teapot or infuser and add boiling water. Allow it to steep for 2 to 5 minutes, depending on the tea. Use the steeping time to meditate on your intention, or use the infusing tea as a focal point for visual or aromatic meditation.

Once the tea has infused, pour it into a teacup and maintain focus as you slowly sip. Visualize the tea's warmth and healing energy radiating throughout your body.

Finish off the ritual by giving gratitude to the tea, your body, and your meditation practice.

Goddess Bath

Water is ultra-supportive of your spiritual and emotional connections and can cleanse unwanted energies that you may be picking up from others around you.

Venus represents all things sensuality, embodiment, and pleasure, the divine feminine archetype proliferating throughout history. We associate Venus with the Roman goddess of love. Still, there are many iterations of this divine feminine archetype in other cultures, from the ancient Egyptians' Isis to the Mesopotamians' Inanna and the Greek equivalent, Aphrodite.

All of these represent sacred and divine power. For this practice, choose the goddess that resonates with you. Feminine energy can be considered yin or lunar energy. There are watery depths in the feminine.

In society, we are often taught to operate from what has traditionally been characterized as an overly masculine space, emphasizing productivity, ambition, and achieving end goals. In contrast, what has been characterized as feminine energy is receptive and flow-oriented without using force to make things happen. If the masculine is like an accelerator in active pursuit, the feminine is a magnet, sitting back and drawing her desires inward.

All of us can use this practice; no matter how you gender identify, the intention is to tap in to your body and your inner magnetism.

Here are a few crystals for the bath and what they're best used for. (**NOTE:** Some crystals don't do well soaking in water, so be sure to research beforehand.)

AMETHYST: Protection and relaxation

ROSE QUARTZ: Self-love and compassion

SMOKEY QUARTZ: Grounding

CITRINE: Balancing, cultivating creativity

CARNELIAN: Increasing libido and sexual energy

HOW TO DO IT

Draw a sacred healing bath by adding your favorite bath salts, dried flowers, and crystals to the water. (If you're short on time or don't have a tub, you can do this practice in the shower; simply shorten up the time in the water.) Have a salt scrub and a floral essential oil like lavender or rose at hand.

Set the intention for your bath. Envision this bath cleansing and healing you on an energetic, physical, spiritual, and emotional level for your highest and greatest good. Bring to mind the energy you wish to cultivate; for example, self-love, grounding, or creativity.

Enjoy soaking for at least 10 to 20 minutes. Water is a conductor of energy and opens connections with your spirit guides and highest self. Be open to receiving whatever messages are in your highest good, and journal afterward about anything that comes up for you.

Once you've had a good soak, exfoliate your skin with a salt scrub, adding a few drops of floral essential oil. Imagine the water purifying you and removing excess emotion from your energetic field as you sit in the bath.

When you finish your bath, visualize old feelings going down the drain with the water. Then, as you emerge from the tub, imagine your own rebirth.

Take a Swim

Whether you live near the ocean, a lake, or a river, or have a local pool you can visit, a vigorous or leisurely swim can invoke healing and transformation and is so good for the body! I grew up as a competitive swimmer until around age twelve, and as I think back on it, those long mornings in the pool were my introduction to meditation.

Swimming provides a space to clear our thoughts while being completely in our body. It's a full-body, low-impact cardio workout that's easy on the joints. It can leave you physically stronger and less likely to experience injuries, with better lung capacity, circulation, and an improved mental state.

If you live near a lake or the ocean, take the opportunity to swim in nature; it is one of the most invigorating experiences. Even if your best option is to go to your local Y or rec center to spend a half hour doing laps, the practice can be incredibly centering.

While swimming, imagine the vast ocean within you. With each breath, notice your life force being replenished and rejuvenated. I love vibrating mantras in my mind while I swim and creating a pattern with my breathing to further the meditative aspect. The goal of a good swim is to end up in a state of delightful exhaustion.

I'M A CURIOUS, ADAPTABLE SEEKER
OF TRUTH. I BREATHE IN A VISION OF
UNIVERSAL LIGHT.

Take a moment to step outside—feel the breeze on your face, listen to the trees rustle and the song of a bird flying up above. Air is all around us. It's that invisible force, filling up our lungs and keeping us alive and well from moment to moment. Air creates motion, energy, and restoration. In wellness practices, air is detoxifying—vinyasa yoga sessions begin with an instruction to take a cleansing breath.

Air is associated with movement—it invokes curiosity, logic, intellectual pursuits, objectivity, and communication. Imaginative, whimsical, adaptable, and intuitive, air is the element of new beginnings, youthful exuberance, and creative bursts of energy. Interpersonal and intellectual pursuits find their home in the ethereal and invisible winds. The air element carries a ubiquitous duality, an omnipresent power whether as a whisper or a hurricane, small talk or deep conversation.

Your elemental constitution is reflected by a variety of factors: your Ayurvedic body type (see page 31), your natal chart and planetary placements, and your surrounding environmental factors. Those with a more predominant constitution of air energy relish learning new things and meeting new people. These are the folks who know how to use their wit and charm in social gatherings and how to maneuver through awkward moments with grace. Air energy influences us to show up as the cool, collected social butterfly: quick-minded, with boundless energy.

When your elemental constitution is balanced and your air energy is in alignment with the other four elements, you may find it easier to cultivate clarity of vision and have the ability to get things done with flair. Conversely, when your air energy is high, you may find yourself feeling scattered, flighty, indecisive, gossipy, and judgmental. If you're experiencing an overdrive of cerebral activity, lying awake at night with worries, consider practices to balance your air energy to find rest and grounding.

Explore locations that allow for treks into cool, open terrains and landscapes, mountaintops, and rolling hills. Air is associated with intellectual pursuits; consider experiences that invoke curiosity, objectivity, and conversation.

THE AIR ELEMENT

ARCHETYPE

Jester, Judge, Teacher

SEASON

Autumn

Autumn is when the winds of change begin to blow. It's the season of preparation and balance. At the onset of the autumnal equinox, when day and night lengths are in perfect equilibrium, we turn inward. In nature, the lushness of summer fades; the leaves change hues, become crisp, and then dance in the wind until the trees are left bare.

LUNAR PHASE

Waxing Moon

The waxing half of the moon's cycle is the perfect time to get creative. The waxing moon's energy is noted as overt, outward, and expanding; it wants you to spring forth and finish what needs to be done to make your dreams a reality. Our energy builds during this moon phase; it's the time of the month to strive to achieve our goals by creating action around our intentions.

CELESTIAL BODY

Jupiter

Jupiter is the bringer of fortune, magic, and luck; it traverses the zodiac slowly, taking twelve years to pass through each sign. It imparts lessons on personal expansion and ideology, and inspires us to continue to learn and grow throughout our lives.

DIRECTION

East

We begin in the east, at sunrise. We arise, take a deep breath, and start our day at first light. The east is associated with the mind, knowledge, and intellectual curiosity. Imagine the birds wheeling overhead; imagine the breeze blowing through your hair. Turning toward the east, we look for a fresh start, an invigorating breath, a new idea.

ASTROLOGICAL SIGNS

Gemini, Libra, Aquarius

Floating through life, leading with their intellect, seemingly free of the clouds of emotion, the air signs are the analysts of the zodiac. It's not that they actually engage mind over emotion; they just process their feelings in their own private way. They're achievers, ideation wizards, and detail keepers.

SENSE

Touch

Air is the giver and receiver of the human touch. Touch is connected to the heart chakra. Deepen your sense of touch by placing your hand on your heart and breathing deeply. Notice how it feels as your heart beats and your chest rises and falls.

NATURE TOOL KIT

AIR PLANTS

ANYTHING
THAT
SYMBOLIZES
A NEW
BEGINNING

COTTON

MICA

FLORITE

TOPAZ

GLASS

BLADES

FEATHER

LAVENDER AND PEPPERMINT
ESSENTIAL OILS

PENS

GLOW

AFFIRMATION

I am a living, breathing example of love.
I'm sensual and royal, a conscious creator.

To honor your relationship with air, return to the basics of self-care: the aroma of a flower and a cool mist on your skin. Experience tension release while encouraging the flow of prana with an ancient Ayurvedic technique, and soak in an ultra-moisturizing bath fit for royalty.

Rose-Infused Facial Mist

In plant mysticism, the rose is said to be the highest vibrational flower. Inhaling the scent of the rose is said to heal the heart, soothe sorrows, and wrap the spirit in divine love. By simply smelling a rose or working with rose water, you are inviting in peace and calm, protection, and high vibrational healing energy, which channels directly into the heart chakra.

In addition to those benefits, rose is an especially wonderful flower for infusing hydration into your skin.

When your air element is out of balance, due to weather conditions or dehydration, you may notice your skin becomes dry and shows signs of fatigue. Women in Bulgaria's Rose Valley, a region that produces over half of the world's rose oil, boil rose petals, strain and cool them, and then apply the water directly to the face to hydrate and refresh the skin. It's a natural anti-aging technique.

Rose has natural astringent qualities as well that can help firm and tone the skin and lighten age spots and blemishes. When there's a predominance of the air element in the weather or in your Ayurvedic constitution, craft your own rose water treatment to deliver hydration and the healing benefits of rose, gently and effectively.

HOW TO MAKE IT

Combine 1 part rose water (found in health food stores or natural grocers) and 1 part witch hazel in a small atomizer. If your skin is especially parched, add a few drops of rose essential oil as well.

Spray on clean skin after you've finished your normal cleansing routine. Let it soak in, and then follow up with a moisturizer. Reapply to refresh and tone the skin throughout the day.

Store your blend in the refrigerator for up to one week. It doesn't keep for long, and it's best used fresh, so make in small batches and discard any leftovers.

Shirodhara-Inspired Oil Treatment

When we have an overabundance of air in our constitution, we can feel flighty and anxious, and our skin loses the ability to retain moisture. I chose this ritual as an air element practice because of its many benefits, including the incredible nourishment and moisture delivered directly to the skin and scalp.

Unlike bodywork therapies that focus on physical manipulation—like, say, a deep-tissue massage—shirodhara primarily works on the mental and internal aspects of your well-being. The word *shirodhara* comes from two Sanskrit words, *shiro* (head) and *dhara* (flow). The practice involves having a warmed herbal oil continuously poured onto your bare forehead while you're lying down. The oil can be streamed in specific patterns related to your dosha type, from the right to the left temple.

After several minutes, the stream is set to the center of the forehead, where it flows uninterrupted. The oil pour also activates a powerful Ayurvedic point between the eyebrows, known as ajna marma or third eye. In Ayurvedic systems, stimulating this point is said to increase the flow of life energy and remove mental, emotional, and spiritual blockages.

The steady stream of warm oil encourages your body to enter a deep state of relaxation—this can help minimize stress-related cortisol levels and convert hyperalert brain patterns (beta waves) into relaxed, alert ones (alpha waves). Shirodhara is also helpful for reducing mental stress, increasing mental clarity, calming anxiety, and improving sleep.

When done regularly, shirodhara or the shirodhara-inspired DIY treatments promote better sleep, enhance blood circulation, nourish the hair and scalp (beauty bonus!), and nuture the mind and body.

HOW TO DO IT

For a shirodhara-inspired experience, gather essential oil, plant oil (like jojoba or almond oil), and a warm, wet washcloth.

Lie down in a comfortable place. Put a drop of lavender, sandalwood, or rose essential oil on the washcloth and drape it over your forehead. Breathe in and relax until the washcloth begins to cool.

Next, rub a few drops of plant oil between your fingertips to warm it, then massage your third eye beneath the washcloth.

Finally, massage your temples and repeat the process until the oil is completely absorbed and you're feeling relaxed and emotionally balanced.

For a more authentic shirodhara experience, warm ½ cup of plant oil for 10 to 15 seconds in the microwave. Lie down with a towel spread beneath your head (to catch excess oil), test the oil temperature with a finger for safety, and with your eyes closed, pour the warmed oil in a steady stream above your third eye center. Once you've finished, massage your third eye point and then simply rest. This practice is especially lovely when shared with a friend. Offer to pour the oil and massage the third eye point for one another for a restorative at-home spa experience.

Cleopatra-Inspired Milk Bath

Cleopatra, the Egyptian queen, is generally depicted as a captivating physical beauty, but in her time she was known as a celebrated intellectual and leader. She spoke as many as a dozen languages and was a mathematics, philosophy, and astronomy scholar.

It's said that Cleopatra was also quite the entrepreneur—owning her own perfumery offering blends from herbs, flower petals, leaves, or seeds mixed with oil from pressed olives. Many of the scents used by the ancient Egyptians—frankincense, myrrh, jasmine, juniper, and cardamom—have endured, making up the key ingredients in popular aromas today.

Perhaps one of the oldest wellness treatments on record is the bath. It's said that Cleopatra is rumored to have often bathed in donkey milk, honey, and essential oils as a part of her beauty ritual. In ancient Egyptian society, bathing with aromatic oils was a daily exercise. Milk calms and moisturizes the skin, vitamins A and E protect it from free radical damage, and B vitamins leave it silky and supple.

In recent times, the art of bathing has returned to its rightful place as a wellness treatment and a luxurious act of self-care. Using ingredients straight from the earth and pH-balancing formulas will keep your body chemistry healthy and your skin soft and hydrated. While Cleopatra was known to bathe in donkey's milk, it isn't as accessible to us as it would have been to a queen, so I've used cow's or goat's milk in this treatment. Feel free to get creative yourself—this is a bath fit for a queen, after all. You can add any other essential oils you feel drawn to—perhaps a few drops of rosemary and peppermint for vitality or lavender for sleep. You can also add a bit of sea salt to enhance detoxification and circulation, and/or olive oil to quench dry skin.

HOW TO DO IT

1 Tbsp raw honey
3 cups cow's or goat's milk, preferably raw
10 drops rose essential oil
A handful of organic fresh or dried rose petals

Fill a bath with comfortably warm water.

Melt the honey in a few cups of water over the stove.

Stir the milk and essential oil into the honey mixture, then add the blend to the bathwater. Add the flower petals as an extra treat. Rose petals raise the energetic frequency of the bath and are said to reduce inflammation and anxious feelings as well.

Soak for up to a half hour and finish the experience with a full-body moisturizer.

GROUND

AFFIRMATION

My breath and inner rhythm flow. I release
habits that hold me back from my highest self.

The air element is our most basic connection to life. Find
grounding through simple yet powerful breathwork and
transcendental meditation. Move energy through the
chakra system to find balance and release negative habits
and patterns.

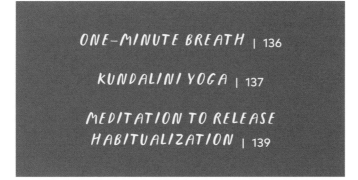

One-Minute Breath

In this pranayama practice, you'll focus on conscious control of the air moving in and out of your body, plus the pace and capacity at which the air flows. This breath takes only a minute, hence the name; however, it's a powerful life force practice, infusing energy into your system. With regular practice of the One-Minute Breath, your lung capacity, focus, and concentration will improve.

In just one sitting, oxygen levels in your blood will begin to rise, increasing your immune capacity, strengthening your circulatory system, and releasing anxious thoughts so your mind can feel at ease. This practice can induce a higher state of consciousness and plentiful, life-changing results.

Be prepared to still your mind and find a deeper connection to your inner voice, as this practice will cultivate a restful silence. The most immediate benefit of this practice is a deep sense of relaxation. You may also notice a release of negative thought patterns and a creative energy boost following the practice.

This breathwork is called the One-Minute Breath because the intention is to grow your lung capacity to a point in which you experience one full rotation of breath in a minute. The practice, in its fullest expression, starts with a 20-second inhale, followed by a suspension of the breath for 20 seconds, and ends with a 20-second exhale. The instructions here introduce the novice to a beginning pace, from which point you can build up to the full minute.

Seat yourself comfortably in a quiet location. Begin with a deep inhale and exhale to settle into the practice.

Set a timer for 1 minute. Inhale for 5 seconds, suspend your breath for 5 seconds, and exhale for 5 seconds. You should complete 4 cycles at this pace. As you repeat this practice, you can gradually lengthen the breath cycle times until you reach the full minute with a single cycle.

Kundalini Yoga

Every morning I show up to my mat, I sit down, and I breathe. I move, I meditate, I get into communion with my body. Because if I don't, the habits and patterns that were infused into my tiny mind and body before I was even seven years old take over. Of all the practices I use to keep myself centered, this is the one I simply can't skip.

When I began practicing kundalini yoga, I realized that I felt better than I ever did in my twenties and thirties. Kundalini yoga is the technology and science of becoming awake and aware while moving through the day-to-day experience of life in an elevated state. A typical kundalini yoga class includes a combination of movement, breath, sound, and chakra healing meditations designed to gently train practitioners to become more conscious of their blocks, both emotionally and physically.

To dedicated practitioners, it's considered a powerful practice that provides deep healing by releasing trauma from the energetic body. If you search the web on kundalini yoga, you'll likely come across yogis dressed in all white, wearing loosely draped outfits and head coverings. You'll find they're chanting specific mantras to "tune in," and while there are traditions in the practice, most teachers will tell you there aren't super strict rules that claim to be "the" way to access oneness and higher purpose, just guiding principles.

When I began my kundalini yoga teacher training with Guru Singh, a celebrated third-generation yogi and master spiritual teacher, he invited his students to experience the practice in a way that's authentic to each of us, which meant wearing what feels comfortable and exploring the mantras, mudras, and kriyas—sets of exercises considered "complete yoga actions"—that most resonated with each of us.

In Sanskrit, *kundalini* means "coiled snake." In early Eastern religions, it was believed that divine energy was created at the base of the spine. Kundalini works to "uncoil the snake" and connect us to our divine energy within. Daily spiritual practice, known as sadhana, enables the kundalini light to rise. The chakra centers open, which supports activating the vagus nerve, the gateway to the parasympathetic nervous system, and strengthening the nervous system.

When our nervous systems are strong, we can process experiences and emotions in a healthy, supported way. Considering that our nervous system affects our sensations, motor control, organs, and limbs as our nerves create connections all through our bodies, it's a system that deserves the highest level of care.

Opening the vagus nerve, coupled with breathwork and mudra work, helps us step out of our egoic mind and lower-vibrational-frequency emotions like envy and frustration and into higher-frequency emotions like love and compassion. We're all human beings, so it's natural for us to cycle through these emotions; in practice, we're choosing to counteract lower-frequency emotional turmoil.

Kundalini yoga is a wonderful practice for beginners and advanced yoga practitioners alike. To get started, sign up for an introductory class in a yoga studio or online. Your first experience can be quite powerful because of the intensity of the breathwork. It's helpful to let your teacher know you're new to the practice so they can offer additional guidance and/or modifications.

Meditation to Release Habitualization

The stories we tell ourselves and our interpretations of what's happening in the world around us substantially impact our perception of reality. Did you know that scientists believe most of our patterns of behavior, our beliefs, and our habits are formed by the age of seven? How we react to day-to-day experiences is completely influenced by the core beliefs we've carried around since we were that young.

These core beliefs encompass how we see ourselves and others and how we understand the actions of the universe. Our subconscious created this system of thinking when we were little kids as we looked to our parents, friends, teachers, and society. As adults, up to 90 percent of our thoughts live in the unconscious realm, and our habits take shape from childhood imprinting.

When something stressful happens at work; when we feel rejected in a dating relationship or by a friend; when we have a disagreement with our partner; when we feel personally attacked when our parents do, well, parent things, some sort of deeply ingrained habitual response is triggered.

Sometimes, our response is vice-like: things like smoking, drinking, or choosing unhealthy foods. Other times, the response is more subtle. For example, we can have addictions to feelings of acceptance, acknowledgment, and advancement, and to specific emotional frequencies, and we can habitualize the behaviors that deliver those feelings and experiences.

This meditation works to repattern the subconscious mind by stimulating the brain area directly underneath the stem of the pineal gland. When the pineal gland is impaired, we can experience hormone imbalance, disruption of sleep, and additional stress triggers. When we have an imbalance in this area, our subconscious habits can seem unbreakable. The meditation allows us to settle our nervous system and show up with ease, presence, clarity, and a sense of purpose.

HOW TO DO IT

Sit on the floor in a traditional cross-legged meditation posture or in a chair if that's more comfortable for you. Straighten your spine; imagine shining your heart outward while pressing your lower back forward.

Make fists with both hands and extend your thumbs straight. Gently place your thumbs on your temples and find the niche where your thumbs fit easily into the space on the side of your head. If you were to look in an anatomy book, this is the lower anterior portion of the frontal bone above the temporal sphenoid suture.

Focus your eyes on your third eye center between your brows. Lightly lock your back molars together and keep your lips sealed. Keeping your teeth pressed together throughout, alternately clench your molars tightly and then release the pressure. The motion should be similar to chewing gum. You'll feel muscles moving in rhythm under your thumbs. Feel a light massage as you continue to hold your thumbs in place.

Once you've got the basics down, you can add this ancient mantra: *Sa Ta Na Ma*. For this meditation, simply vibrate the mantra in your mind. Sa is birth and the beginning, ta is the creative expression of our lives, na is the transformation of consciousness, and ma is our regeneration. Continue the meditation for 3 minutes to begin, working up to 30 minutes of meditation. It may feel quite unusual at first, but this is the type of meditation that will work wonders with a few minutes a day of regular practice.

NOURISH

AFFIRMATION

Through the power of my practice,
transformations are happening in me.

Learn to make your own spiced tea to settle the body and mind. Tuck spirit tools into your pillow to find inner peace and quiet, and take a walk outdoors for a daily dose of vitamin D.

Make Homemade Chai

The chai you find in nearly any coffeehouse today has quite a history. Chai is steeped in the lore of royalty and herbal medicine. The word *chai* is derived from the Chinese word for tea—*cha*. There are records of chai being served in royal courts in India and Siam (now Thailand) as far back as nine thousand years ago. Native tea plants have been used by South Asians as herbal medicine since ancient times, purported to cure simple disorders such as the common cold and digestive ailments.

Today, across India, you will find chai being stirred by chai wallahs, tea vendors, on crowded streets and ladled out of simmering pots in household kitchens. Over thousands of years, recipes have been passed between families, villages, cities, and countries, and no matter how you take yours—sweet, spicy, or creamy—chai is a universal offering that transcends.

I especially love chai to help me settle after traveling. The warming spices, specifically ginger, are nice for a queasy stomach. If you're adjusting to a new time zone, the combination of caffeine and L-theanine offers a mental boost.

I visited one of my favorite restaurants in the world— Dishoom in London—years ago and had the most aromatically complex and delicious tea that evening. The next day while wandering the Old Spitalfields Market, I came across a chai wallah, ordered a cup, and decided if I couldn't take this moment home with me, I could at least learn to make my own chai at home.

My recipe includes ginger; I love the soothing, healing qualities it brings. However, feel free to adjust your spices and blend according to your personal taste!

HOW TO MAKE IT

Makes 2 to 3 cups

> 1 cinnamon stick
> 1 tsp whole black peppercorns
> 5 whole cloves
> 5 cardamom pods
> 1 to 2 cups cold water, depending on simmer time
> 3 bags Darjeeling tea
> 2 cups milk
> 1 in piece of ginger, thinly sliced
> Honey for sweetening

Crush the spices with a large spoon. Add the ginger and muddle (I recommend starting with a few slices of ginger and then adding more to taste if needed). Transfer the spices and ginger to a saucepan and add 1 to 2 cups of water. Use more water if you intend to simmer the spices longer.

Bring the water to a boil over high heat, then reduce to low and bring to a simmer. Let simmer for at least 10 minutes, but up to 1 to 2 hours for a spicier flavor.

Once the spices have become aromatic and incorporated, add the tea bags and steep for 5 minutes.

Remove the tea bags, add the milk and honey, and let the whole mixture come to a simmer for just a moment to blend. Strain the chai into a teapot or mugs and serve.

Sleep with a Medicine Pillow

If you find yourself tossing and turning at night and in need of something to bring on sweet dreams and restful slumber, creating your own medicine pillow will guide you into a peaceful night's repose.

HOW TO DO IT

A medicine pillow is a small silk or cotton pouch that you can fill with any combination of herbs, oils, and crystals, then tuck it into your regular pillow. Depending on what sort of feeling and energy you're interested in cultivating, you can experiment with different combinations to create the pillow that best suits you.

Choose your additions. Here are some suggestions based on the experience you'd like to cultivate:

HERBS: lavender for sleep, mugwort or rosemary to stimulate vivid dreaming, bay leaf or thyme to release stress, or oregano or chamomile for peace and relaxation.

CRYSTALS: For sleep, try howlite, amethyst, moonstone, rose quartz, and lepidolite. To encourage dreaming, try clear quartz, celestine, labradorite, or moldavite. If you have insomnia, hematite, cookeite, and red or Dalmatian jasper can induce sleepiness and bring about a feeling of tranquility, helping you fall asleep and stay asleep until it's time to wake up. Before creating your medicine pillow, charge your crystals in moonlight (see page 110), setting the intention for peaceful sleep.

Once you've chosen your herbs and crystals, add them to the pouch with a few drops of bergamot, rose, or lavender oil. Wrap it all up and place it inside your pillow. You can leave the medicine pillow inside your pillow for a few days at a time, refilling the pouch if you find the herbs losing their aroma or the essential oils dissipating. Remember to recharge your crystals each full moon with a moon bath to release any energy they're holding.

Take a Brisk Morning Walk

I have a yoga teacher who often shares the old adage "How you do anything is how you do everything" with the students in class. I love it as a reminder to consider the integrity of how we show up even when no one is watching. Although I may not set my alarm clock for 5 a.m. each morning, I love the concept presented in Robin Sharma's book *The 5 AM Club: Own Your Morning. Elevate Your Life.* The idea is to rise early and commit to 20 minutes of exercise, 20 minutes of planning, and 20 minutes of study before beginning your daily tasks.

How we start the day sets the tone for what's to come. Personally, my Ayurvedic-inspired morning ritual, plus 15 minutes of meditation, is the first thing I do when I get out of bed. In addition, it helps to hold me accountable for staving off the phone scroll until after meditation is complete and ensures I consider my health before doing anything else.

No matter whether you find it easy to pop up out of bed first thing in the morning or routinely struggle with the snooze button, adding in a brisk morning walk to help you get the day started is a simple and effective wellness ritual available to most of us no matter our location.

Regardless of your level of fitness or body type, getting outside at first light, feeling the dew on your skin, and filling up your lungs with the morning air is truly one of the easiest ways to improve your well-being. A brisk morning walk, in which your breath is deep and forceful yet purposeful and sustainable, will boost your brainpower, as you're optimizing cerebral blood flow and your metabolism while burning energy. It will work wonders on your energy level, your productivity, and even your sleep patterns.

Sunlight is a powerful stimulus for supporting your levels of alertness throughout the day and for inspiring better sleep at night. Timing is key. Absorbing bright light through outdoor exposure first thing in the morning will enhance your well-being all day long. Simply head outside to walk with intention (with a watch so you can keep it to 20 minutes). Tuck your phone away or leave it behind. Focus on your breath, allow your mind to relax, and perhaps spend a few moments visualizing the day ahead while you move.

Whether you have access to a trail or simply enjoy a jaunt around your neighborhood, making this practice a part of your daily routine will brighten your mood and enhance your health, creativity, and longevity. If you don't have access to sunlight or if it's too cold to be outside for long, consider an indoor sun lamp and 10 to 20 minutes of indoor movement as an alternative.

I'M AN INTUITIVE AND DIVINE BEING,
A TRAVELER OF THE QUANTUM REALMS.

The ether element (akasha in Sanskrit) refers to space, the infinity of the cosmos, and the heavens. It is believed that everything above the sky is ethereal, made of ether. It's where our spiritual journey begins. The scientist Carl Sagan famously reminded us, "We are star stuff"—the most essential elements of life, the building blocks that make up our being, are the same as what's found in the cosmos. We're all energy, we're all connected, and when we align with each of the earthly elements, as well as the stars in the sky, we can truly make magic happen.

In medieval times, the Latin phrase *prima materia* referred to the formless root of all matter, the mother of all things—a blend of stars and soil, the totality of how we began, and an essential component in the alchemical magnum opus.

Ether, unlike the other elements, is based more on the absence of its opposing quality. Ether is dark, cold, and quiet because it lacks warmth and energy created by fire. It's weightless because it lacks the heaviness created by the earth. It's still because it lacks the propulsive nature of air and water. It's subtle, yet omnipresent.

Ether is associated with intuition, insight, future sight, and the deepest knowledge in the spiritual sense. Just as animals know when the weather is going to change, humans too have this special sense, an extrasensory perception carried in the atmosphere.

There is no season, lunar phase, time of day, or astrological sign associated with ether. Ether is all-encompassing and nothingness at the same time. It's infinity, inclusive of all sunrises and sunsets through eternity.

Regarding the five senses, ether is the medium through which sound is transmitted; thus, the ethereal element is related to our auditory perception. A daily practice of chanting opens the vagus nerve. Creating and experiencing specific frequencies allows us to tune in to our own micro orbit.

Sound waves that travel through ether can induce a state of ease in the body. The yoga science of melody and rhythm is known as Naad Brahm, the sacred music of life, and Shabd Guru, the teachings of sound, which makes up the supreme nature of harmony. The vibration of mantra holds life inside of time, serving as the connection between the heavens and the earth, between the body and the soul.

Exploring cosmic practices, working with crystals—specifically gemstones from space—and tapping into modalities that allow you to move through the day-to-day experience of life at an elevated state are what's on the menu in this chapter.

For those who love to wander, experiencing our planet's extremities—volcanoes, vast deserts, or the deep sea, for example—or visiting a planetarium to learn more about the stars can connect you to the bigger picture of our universal reality.

NATURE TOOL KIT

FOSSIL

TAROT DECK

AMETHYST

ROCK WATER
FLOWER ESSENCE

LOTUS FLOWER TEA

SACRED INCENSE

MOONSTONE

PETRIFIED WOOD

A BOTTLE OF SAND

QUARTZ

LABRADORITE CRYSTALS

GLOW

AFFIRMATION

I'm an authentic being of grace, divinely guided,
channeling the energy of the muse.

To create a cosmic glow, these practices include invoking
ancient goddess energy, creating a hair mask from a storied
divine root, and tapping into the energies of extraterrestrial
crystals. They also encourage a graceful approach to beauty
and wellness, minimal effort, and simple yet supernatural
techniques.

Cosmic Swan Breathing

There's an ancient Greek story regarding the birth of Helen of Troy, daughter of Zeus and Leda. Helen was known to be the most beautiful woman in Greece, and her conception was quite unusual. It's said that to win the affection of Leda, Zeus transformed himself into a swan. The encounter became a potent subject for artists in ancient Greece and Renaissance Italy, inspiring art by da Vinci, Michelangelo, Giampietrino, and Tintoretto, to name a few.

The constellation Cygnus ("swan" in Latin), cataloged by the Greek astronomer Ptolemy, is still visible in the night sky. While there are several mythological origins associated with this constellation, including the story of Zeus's transformation, Cygnus always represents the mystery, grace, and glow of the cosmic swan. In a dark sky, you can imagine Cygnus flying along the starlit trail of the summer Milky Way.

Cosmic swan breathing is a beauty practice shared by ancient yogis with the intention of quickly and effectively infusing the skin with a glowing vibrancy while guiding you into an illuminated state of being.

This practice opens up the vertebrae, flushes the brain with cerebral spinal fluid, and oxygenates the blood. In addition, it's known to refresh the capillaries, giving the cheeks a rosy hue.

I like to think of this practice as both a glow and grace amplifier.

Start by sitting on your heels in rock pose (kneeling, with a cushion tucked beneath your backside to avoid overextending your knees), and placing your hands on the floor on either side of your knees. If this posture is unavailable to you, sitting in a chair is another option. Sit gracefully; imagine you are a swan floating along a glistening lake.

Begin rounding your spine and the back of your neck over, tucking your chin into your chest. Bow your head to the floor. Inhale and swoop your torso forward, like a swan diving into water, arching your back and putting the total weight of your upper body on the tops of your thighs. Keep your hands planted on the floor on either side of your body.

Once you've completed the dive, exhale as you stretch forward and then return to your original position. The movement is an undulation of the spine: rounding, arching, and stretching.

End this sequence seated upright again, now resting both hands in your lap, eyes closed, like a swan floating gracefully along the water.

As recommended with other breathwork practices in this book, try to commit to 3 minutes daily; with this specific practice, the vitality benefits of the movement come from the pumping of cerebrospinal fluid through your system. The cerebrospinal fluid does lots of things: It aids the body in producing more collagen, which can result in improved hydration and elasticity in our skin.

He Shou Wu Hair Mask

Originally grown in China, *he shou wu* (*Reynoutria multi-flora*; common names are tuber fleeceflower and Chinese knotweed), one of the most popular tonic herbs in Chinese herbalism, translates as "the black hair of Mr. He." The name comes from the legend of a man who'd fallen very ill; he'd lost his energy and begun losing his hair. He traveled into the forest to find healing, and while there, came across a flowering vine with a woody tuber. He experienced a divine download, a vision from above.

From that vision, Mr. He decided to make a tea from the root, and as he drank the tea, his hair, his youthful vitality, and his life force began to return. Since then, he shou wu has become a staple in traditional Chinese medicine.

There are many ways to work with the herb; for our recipe, we'll be using it in powder form in conjunction with bhring-araj oil to make a hair mask. He shou wu is known to return color to graying hair, and when taken orally (try cooking he shou wu with black beans—its flavor is earthy and slightly sweet), it's said to be a powerful anti-aging ingredient. Bhringaraj oil comes from false daisy (*Eclipta prostrata*) and is used in Ayurvedic tradition to promote hair growth and retain hair color. The nutrients in the oil facilitate blood flow to the hair follicles while nourishing the scalp.

As we age and experience hormonal shifts, it's normal for our hair to feel more brittle and lose its luster. This mask will help with hydration and density, plus it can promote melanin production, which can help revitalize your mane if you're experiencing hair loss or graying.

1 Tbsp he shou wu powder
1 tsp bhringaraj oil
1 Tbsp coconut oil

In a small saucepan over medium heat, combine ¼ cup of water with the he shou wu powder and stir until the powder becomes a paste. Add the bhringaraj and coconut oils and stir to fully incorporate. Transfer to a small bowl.

Gently massage the warm mask into your scalp in a circular motion for about 15 minutes (having a partner do this for you is a special treat) and leave it in your hair for another 30 minutes. To finish the treatment, shampoo and condition your hair with a mild natural cleanser and moisturizer. It's recommended to use the he shou wu mask once a week.

Gemstone Facial Sculpting

Amethyst, howlite, clear quartz, moonstone, carnelian, and azurite are common crystals associated with space. Working with ether element healing gems, crystals, and stones elevates our human energetics to higher realms. In addition, some space gemstones, also known as extra-terrestrial gemstones, have origins traced to deep in the cosmos:

Moldavite formed when an asteroid hit the earth fifteen million years ago.

Space peridot, also known as the sun gem or evening emerald, was discovered by ancient Egyptians; the rarest source of peridot is from meteorites that have broken off from a planet or asteroid.

Opals were found by the Mars Rover in 2015; a year later, a meteorite studded with pieces of opal was discovered in Antarctica.

Working with these gems is said to ease vertigo, dizziness, headaches, and claustrophobia; they're known to improve cognitive functioning and memory as well.

Use of gemstones as beauty tools dates back to the ancient Chinese, Egyptians, and Mayans. Rolling specific stones along facial pressure points was believed to soothe stressed organs, flush out impurities, and slow down the process of cellular aging. This practice is also said to increase chi, revitalizing energy that has the power to rejuvenate and renew facial muscles for a radiant complexion.

When we work with these stones for facial sculpting, we add another layer of holistic healing to our beauty practice. Facial rollers, wands, and gua sha tools stimulate blood flow and drain stagnant lymph via targeted sculpting movements. Regular facial rolling is like a workout for your face: As you slide your tool along each section of your face, you'll release tension, tone muscles, firm the skin, and reduce puffiness. After incorporating this practice into your daily routine, expect more definition in your cheekbones and jawline.

Gua sha is a traditional East Asian and Chinese technique, predating acupuncture. The stroke pattern used by gua sha technicians awakens the meridian lines to activate the body's natural healing abilities.

It inspires radiance by increasing circulation, sending nutrients to areas that may have been depleted because of blockages. Working with a volcanic rock or amethyst gua sha, the most popular etheric element crystal, will provide a beautiful sculpting effect while helping to detoxify the skin and mind.

HOW TO DO IT

Start by applying a layer of facial mist or oil, so your tool will have some slip as you sculpt.

Begin to sculpt. Breathe deeply, and move slowly as you sculpt, stroking each area of the face and neck for a count of seven. Make sure to pull up with your tool gently, never pushing or dragging the skin downward (we're working against gravity with this practice). Use both hands, one to pull the tool upward, one to support the skin. Keep the tool at a 15- to 45-degree angle to maximize the contact between the tool and your skin.

For the best results, sculpt each evening before bedtime and then apply a light moisturizer.

GROUND

AFFIRMATION

I belong in this world. I'm a seeker
of truth and curiosity.

To find your footing here on Earth, explore the power of
vibrational frequencies, host a manifestation circle, and
look to the cosmos for intuitive guidance. Study astronomy
and astrology and let your imagination, focus, and intention
shape your energy.

Sound Healing

There are vibrational frequencies that correspond to every-thing in the universe. Love, happiness, joy, envy, and regret, for example, are vibratory frequencies. Since ancient times, music and mantra have been recognized for their ability to heal. Different frequencies of sound have different effects on human brain activity.

Our brains naturally sync to specific tone scales, like the ancient Gregorian chants (also known as the solfeggio frequencies). Singing these ancient chants or listening to these frequencies ranging from 174 Hz to 963 Hz is known to have all sorts of wellness benefits, from evoking feelings of love and courage to dissolving feelings of trauma and encouraging clear communication.

Much of the technology of our modern world disrupts the natural earth frequencies. In yogic technologies, Sahaj Shabd ("the ease of harmonic sound") is a therapeutic technique that uses tones and melodies to align with our intuitive consciousness.

In his major treatise *De Anima* (On the Soul), Aristotle described the flute as an instrument that could evoke an emotional response and purify the soul. Greek physicians used flutes and lyres to heal patients, connecting to the power of vibrational frequencies to aid digestion, treat mental disturbance, and promote sleep. Native Americans, First Nations, and other Indigenous communities work with song, chanting, and drums as a community wellness modality and healing rite.

Today's sound healing can include gong meditation, mantra, and chanting in a yoga class or ceremonial ritual, listening to binaural beats, experiencing tuning forks, or creating a sound bath with singing bowls. As I sit and write, I alternate between playing kundalini mantras for creativity and chakra healing frequencies to improve my focus and motivation.

As a form of meditation, sound baths are a beautiful way to drop deeply into meditative serenity. Our brains naturally begin to synchronize with the rhythm of the music in these practices, so as the calming rhythms begin, our mind moves into a slower wave state. Some of the most common sound bath instruments are:

Chimes
Gongs
Tuning forks
Singing bowls
Harps

In my experience, whether I'm in a yoga studio experiencing crystal singing bowls or listening to the gong while I sleep, I find the vibrations flow through me and move me quickly into a relaxed, restful, and even trancelike state in which the worries of the day float away. There's a natural energy cleansing that happens through sound.

I started listening to a couple of specific gong frequencies while sleeping years ago. Created by the Grammy Award–winning musical group White Sun, the two songs I love are called "Healing Gong" and "Wish-Fulfilling Gong."

I also love chanting mantras in my daily meditation practices.

I once heard a yoga master say that when she began chanting mantras, all of the swirling thoughts in her mind instantly disappeared. I loved that explanation of the healing power of sound, and I encourage you to try it. When it comes to selecting a mantra, the choices are infinite. I often choose a mantra from my kundalini yoga practice, "Ong namo guru dev namo" ("I bow to the teacher within").

You could also use short affirmation statements as your mantra. For example: "I am bountiful," "I am blissful," "I am beautiful." Once you've selected the mantra, repeat the chant in your mind or out loud. Continue for 3 minutes as a part of your regular practice, and even 10 minutes or more as you have time.

When we chant a mantra, we invoke the resonance and power within the syllables. Whether it's for abundance, peace of mind, or increased intuition, we are setting vibrations in motion.

Host a Moon Manifestation Circle

I started studying manifestation and the law of attraction in 2006 (coincidentally, the same year a documentary exploring these topics, called *The Secret*, came out, followed by Rhonda Byrne's companion book of the same title). I noticed that the approach was working, so I studied everything about the concept of manifestation that I could get my hands on. The more I refined my process, the more I experienced serendipitous encounters.

Today, I teach courses on the topic, guiding my students through the basics of manifestation and giving them the tools to take inspired action and design blueprints of their future. Manifestation isn't exclusively saying positive affirmations over and over again and has nothing to do with superstition. It involves exploring your beliefs about what's possible while learning to work with your emotional state and vibrational frequency. It's about creating a vision, leaning into the emotions associated with that vision, and then taking inspired action to bring your vision and feelings to life.

A Moon Manifestation Circle can technically be hosted at any time of the month, during any phase of the month. It's wise to consider what sort of energy you're interested in cultivating when planning your circle. Lunar forces are invisible; however, just as the moon affects the tides, our bodies can feel the energetic shifts.

The new moon is a time to rest, regenerate, and go inward. If you're hosting your circle around this lunar phase, it's a beautiful time to reflect and set your goals for the month ahead. The sky is dark on a new moon, resembling a blank canvas and a time of fresh potential. During a new moon ceremony, spend time pondering and refining your intentions as you consider what you want to manifest.

If you're hosting a Full Moon Manifestation Circle, it's a wonderful time to get specific about your dreams. First, write a list of what you're calling into your life. Then take time to celebrate and express gratitude. Gratitude is a brilliant practice to amplify and supercharge your manifestation energy.

Gather a group of friends—the most important component of the experience is the connection time.

Create a ceremony that resonates with your group, allowing time for meditation, chanting, and journaling. Here are a few ideas to get you started: build a moon altar together, perform a warming tea ritual (page 114), make ritual water under the light of the moon (page 110), charge your crystals (page 110), or practice a fire-releasing ritual (page 52).

Above all, focus on being in the present moment, and enjoy the experience of existing in communion with others, raising your vibrational frequency together. As you work toward your dreams, notice and acknowledge that small shifts can lead to momentous transformation over time.

Study Your Astrological Chart

One of the first steps in any cosmic journey is to understand your astrological natal chart. For most of us, it begins with our sun sign, the main sign you look up in astrology columns and identify when someone asks that cocktail party question, "What's your sign?"

As you begin to deepen your astrological knowledge, you'll quickly find more to your natal chart than just your sun sign. The key areas most astrologers will start with during a reading are your "big three": sun, moon, and rising signs. These have the most influence over how we show up in our day-to-day life.

Next, you'll take a look at which houses the planets are in. The houses rule the key areas of our lives, ranging from work and relationships to sex, money, and death. So having an understanding of the houses will further your overall knowledge of your chart.

There are all sorts of other themes to uncover in a chart reading; for example, where your North Node lies projects what your purpose is in this lifetime; the minor planet Chiron, which was added to astrology in the 1970s, shows where you may need healing; and your Venus placement speaks to how you love and like to be loved.

While astrology isn't a science, there's a long history of humans looking up to the cosmos for life guidance. In ancient times, farmers used the skies as a calendar for planting and harvesting their crops, travelers used the constellations as a compass, and people of many cultures looked to the stars for mystical guidance.

When booking an astrology reading, you can request a general reading, including a conversation on the overarching themes based on your planetary placements. If there are specific topics you have an interest in—career or love, for example—a reader could specifically speak to those areas as well.

What's important is to go into your astrology reading with an open mind. Remember that this isn't about predicting your future or deciphering a hard-and-fast fate; it's simply a guiding tool to open pathways to higher alignment with yourself and how you show up in the world. Allow the process to be one of expansion and learning.

NOURISH

AFFIRMATION

I'm connected to transcendental visions,
living with mindful integrity.

Nourishment comes in many forms. It's what we take in via food and drink; the oils and herbs we soak in and the creams we delicately apply to our skin. And just like our bodies, our intuition needs nourishment too. To connect to higher realms, listen to our inner wisdom, and invite divine downloads to channel through us, consider these practices to nourish the third eye and the body's meridian points. Restore your energy's natural rhythm and balance with a brew, a meditative activation, and an acupuncture-like technique you can do anywhere.

Brew Blue Lotus Tea

The blue lotus (*Nymphaea caerulea*) is an ethnobotanical gem that has been highly regarded through the ages as the "Flower of Enlightenment" or "Sacred Lily of the Nile." It's a sacred flower best known for its powers of intuition, rejuvenation, and aphrodisia. There are traditions dedicated to this plant that go back forty thousand years within recorded botanical scripts.

Among the ancient temples of Egypt, there is hardly a monument to be found that doesn't prominently display the blue lotus flower. It's seen everywhere on pillars, thrones, stone altars, papyrus scrolls, and the ceremonial headdresses of pharaohs. When Tutankhamun's tomb was discovered, they found that even King Tut's mummy was covered in this special blossom.

So important was the blue lotus to ancient Egyptians that it was said that consuming the flower would invoke the gods above. The plant is associated with the sun god Ra, the bringer of light and the embodiment of the "perfection of wisdom." Often used in funerary ceremonies after the death of a loved one, the blue lotus is said to encourage the soul to enter the light.

Traditional Aboriginal medicine in Australia includes the blue lotus as well. The blue lotus offers a calming and euphoric sensation believed to release fears and increase states of cosmic connection and ultimate soul growth.

Boil enough water for a mug (or two if you're sharing with a friend).

Add 2 Tbsp of dried blue lotus flowers to a tea strainer or infuser and immerse in hot water. Steep for 5 to 10 minutes. Add honey to taste, then strain the blue lotus flower tea into your favorite mug and serve.

As you sip, consider this as more than just a cup of tea: It is a system reset and an intuition-activating beverage.

Third Eye Activation

Many meditation or yoga practices use the third eye, or the sixth chakra, as a focal point. By bringing the eyes to focus on the space between the eyebrows, we stimulate the subconscious mind and our intuitive channels. The intention is to activate the pituitary gland and see beyond what is physically present in the moment.

The sixth chakra is the ajna chakra. *Ajna* means "command" or "authority." Through the ajna and pituitary gland, we can learn to have authority and command over our mindset. The third eye allows us to have a clear perception of our reality, to better understand our purpose in life. When our sixth chakra is awakened, we have a reliable intuition and can see the unseen.

The consistent focus at the physical location of this energetic center is potent—some people may even experience visions and clairvoyance when their third eye is activated. Whether or not that occurs for you, this practice increases clarity and provides new ways of viewing the world around you.

HOW TO DO IT

Find a comfortable, calm, and private place where you can meditate without being disturbed.

Settle in and start to focus on your breath. Take deep breaths through your nose, holding the air in for a few seconds and exhaling through your mouth. Don't force your breathing; follow the natural rhythm of your body. Visualize each breath as a healing and soothing energy entering your body, and each exhale as a cloud carrying away the thoughts and experiences you're ready to let go of. If your mind wanders, simply come back to your breath.

As you deepen your breathing, fill your lungs to full capacity, feeling the air expand your chest up to your collarbones.

Now start to activate your third eye. Keeping your eyes closed, roll them upward so they're "looking" between your eyebrows. Next, raise your eyebrows so your forehead is crinkled. Hold your gaze right on that spot between your brows. Then relax your eyebrows.

Imagine relaxing the crown of your head, the sides of your head, and the back of your head, and if your tongue has crept up to the roof of your mouth, let it drop and relax.

As you hold your gaze on your third eye energy center, visualize a tiny indigo light taking shape. Focus your gaze on this light. Continue to focus, and breathe long and deep.

After several minutes, release the focus and the intentional deep breathing and open your eyes. At the close of your practice, take time to journal about your experience. Notice what clarity arises for you, what ideas or visions have come to mind. Spend time exploring this awareness as you journal. You may find that downloads or divine hits continue to surface hours after your practice. Pay close attention to what continues to come up for you. You can make this activation a daily practice to enhance creativity, support decision-making, and find emotional balance.

EFT Tapping

Psychological acupressure, also called emotional freedom technique (EFT), was introduced by Gary Craig in 1993. He believed that blocked or disrupted energy was the root cause of all negative emotions we experience. For example, early in my career, I traveled weekly, in and out of airports, surrounded by lots of energy and emotions. As an empath, I found I was taking on other people's energy, and in turn, my own anxieties were amplified.

I was introduced to EFT by my therapist. I'd shared with her that the emotional energy I was picking up, plus my own feelings of being out of control while flying, led to what was becoming a pretty intense fear of flying. I learned the basics of EFT Tapping in her office and then began to apply what I'd learned, practicing a basic sequence, every time I headed to the airport. The results were remarkable: The next time I had a flight, by using EFT I immediately felt the fear leave my body.

EFT Tapping is based on disciplines such as tai chi and acupuncture; tapping focuses on the meridian points of the body to restore the natural rhythm and balance of our energy.

HOW TO DO IT

To learn simple EFT techniques, find reputable teachers online and watch videos, following along with the sequences. To go even further, seek a professional practitioner.

Here is my typical EFT sequence:

STATEMENT: State your emotions out loud; consider, on a scale of 0 to 10 (0 being relaxed and completely calm, and 10 being totally scared and anxious), how you're feeling, recognizing where you may be troubled.

SET-UP: Create a phrase that explains your goal. This sentence must focus on acknowledging the issue and accepting yourself despite the problem. A typical set-up phrase might be: *Even though I am/I have _____ (fill in the blank with the emotion you're experiencing), I deeply and completely accept/love myself.*

With two fingers, start gently tapping on the ends of your meridian points—between your eyebrows, sides of your eyes, under your nose, chin, collarbones, and arms. As you tap, repeat your set-up phrase over and over and focus on your desired outcome.

At the end of the sequence, rate your level of emotional concern again on a scale of 0 to 10. Keep repeating this sequence until your level reaches a significantly lower number than what you started with.

ACKNOWLEDGMENTS

Thank you to my many teachers, guides, and mentors, specifically those who've contributed to my wellness journey. What a gift it's been to learn from you and your experiences. To all the individuals I have had the opportunity to share these practices with, I'm eternally indebted; you are the inspiration and foundation for this book.

Much gratitude to Kim Perel, my agent, for believing in me and the importance of these well-being practices; my editor Cristina Garces for your friendship, enthusiasm, and steadfast support, especially when the world got weird; and Madeline Martinez, for your illustrations that brought next-level magic to these pages. You each have my deepest thanks.

To everyone on the Chronicle team, including Jessica Ling, Lizzie Vaughan, Angie Kang, Gabby Vanacore, Janine Sato, Kristi Hein, and Diane João, your dedication and contributions are so appreciated.

Having a concept for a book and allowing it to ebb and flow is akin to the human experience; there are moments of darkness and light. I especially want to thank my team at *Oui, We* for giving me space to work on this project while keeping things moving, specifically Samantha Miker, Adaire Smithwick, and Drew Porrett, as well as my husband, Ben Alleman.

Thank you to Debra Neill and family for being a part of my path to Ayurvedic beauty; to Guru Singh, Kundalini University, and Benshen course for my yoga schooling; and to Chelsea Jewel, Elisabeth McKinley, Fatima-Zahra Farahate, and Mackenzie Greer for a deeper understanding of astrology.

Thank you to all the bookstores, boutiques, and wellness studios that have been willing to put this book on your shelves. I cherish the prime real estate you've given me. Lastly, thank you to the readers. I'm cheering you on; I feel blessed to be on this journey together.